Connecting with Young People in Trouble

Risk, Relationships and Lived Experience

Connecting with Young People in Trouble: Risk, Relationships and Lived Experience
Andi Brierley

ISBN 978-1-909976-89-4 (Paperback)
ISBN 978-1-909976-90-0 (Epub ebook)
ISBN 978-1-909976-91-7 (Adobe ebook)

Cover design © 2021 Waterside Press: www.gibgob.com and with the kind assistance of Tamara Gomez.

Main UK distributor Gardners Books, 1 Whittle Drive, Eastbourne, BN23 6QH. Telephone +44 (0)1323 521777; sales@gardners.com; www.gardners.com

North American distribution Ingram Book Company, One Ingram Blvd, La Vergne, TN 37086, USA. Telephone (+1) 615 793 5000; inquiry@ingramcontent.com

Cataloguing In-Publication Data A catalogue record for this book can be obtained from the British Library.

Printed by Severn, Gloucester, UK.

Ebook *Connecting with Young People in Trouble* is available as an ebook including via library models.

Published 2021 by
Waterside Press Ltd
Sherfield Gables
Sherfield on Loddon, Hook
Hampshire RG27 0JG.

Telephone +44 (0)1256 882250
Online catalogue WatersidePress.co.uk
Email enquiries@watersidepress.co.uk

Royalties from the first 1,000 copies of this work go to support Martin House Hospice Care for Children and Young People (Charity No. 517919).

Connecting with
Young People in Trouble

Risk, Relationships and Lived Experience

Andi Brierley

Foreword Lisa Cherry

❈ WATERSIDE PRESS

Table of Contents

Publisher's note

The views and opinions in this book are those of the author and not necessarily shared by the publisher. Readers should draw their own conclusions concerning the possibility of alternative views, accounts, descriptions or explanations.

Further disclaimer
The author states: 'Although I am currently an employee of Leeds City Council, this book is a collection of my personal views and experiences combined with research readily available for public consumption. The ideas, views and perspectives are not endorsed or collaborated in by my employer in any way and therefore do not reflect Leeds City Council's objectives, values or operations.'

Acknowledgments

Many people have contributed to this book, either wittingly or not. There are so many professionals that have provided me with insights into their work and knowledge and, without them, I would not have been able to learn, develop and provide these considered reflections or observations and make a hopefully positive contribution to youth justice practice. Dr Daniel Siegal, Dr Sean Creaney, Dr Nadine Burke Harris, Dr Gabor Mate, Dr Bessel Van Der Kolk, Dr Bruce Perry, Dr Karen Treisman and Lisa Cherry have been instrumental in my own personal and professional development. Also, so many Leeds professionals have supported me in one way or another after providing me with the opportunity to make a difference to the lives of young people caught up in my previous life circumstances. Thank you to Katie Wrench, Denis Lewis, Steve Walker and Trevor Woodhouse, as well as so many others because, to me, Leeds is the best city for inclusion and investing in people. Several other inspirational people have supported me throughout this journey such as James Docherty, Darren Coyne, Kevin Neary, Dr Beth Weaver and Alex O'Donnell. All have shone their light on me and I can't thank them enough. Last but far from least in terms of youth justice, Andrew, Atticus and Luke (*Chapter 6*, 'Joint Enterprise') for their incredible insights and contributions.

I would also like to thank Martin House Hospice Care for Children and Young People to which I have donated my royalties from the first 1,000 copies of this work.

On a more personal note, I would like to thank my wife Tamara who has supported me throughout the production of this book during the Covid-19 crisis. I had wanted to write of the thoughts and reflections I have had for some time and share my practice experiences of relationship building. Writing this book has taken the most toll on Tamara and our daughter Isabelle. My mind being focused on it alongside working full-time in a children's home while tackling the pandemic means the sacrifice has been as much theirs as it has mine. They are my rock and motivation and for the next few years, at least, no more additional work projects, he says with a smile on his face.

Andi Brierley, January 2021

About the author

Andrew (Andi) Brierley is a Youth Justice Specialist and former prisoner. He has 15 years of experience gained from working with some of the most prolific, serious, vulnerable and complex children and young people involved in offending behaviour, building trusting relationships and connections with many young people that have been identified as 'hard to reach.' He has a track record of making a difference using his own personal experiences mixed with professional knowledge and insight. His lived experience of complex trauma and adverse childhood experiences (which unfortunately for him and others developed into his care experience, school exclusion, drug addiction, criminal exploitation and incarceration) now shape his practice and connections with children and families. He is the author of *Your Honour Can I Tell You My Story?* (Waterside Press, 2019), his autobiography in which he was driven to write about those experiences, and which has already made a difference for other children, young people in trouble or incarcerated and professionals working with them. *Connecting With Young People in Trouble: Risk, Relationships and Experience* builds on that earlier work so as to allow readers to far better understand the relational issues many such youngsters experience—and how they can 'bounce back.'

Foreword

Once it is truly understood that humans are interdependent and need one another, then there become resounding consequences for service policy, provision and practice; the knowledge that we thrive on connection, attunement and resonance should be at the centre of all we do. Ultimately, this is Brierley's call to action as he takes the reader on a journey around the impact of relational poverty, the importance of the quality of 'the village' and the consequences of toxic stress. He calls upon all those working in all aspects of criminal justice to be curious, to look beyond what is standing in front of them and to become relational activists in our approach towards the young people who need us to work towards diminishing harm rather than be part of a system that adds to it.

This book sits at the intersection between personal lived experience and professional practice and as such this makes it a hugely valuable contribution to the discourse. In recent times, an expectation that the voices of children and young people in care are taken into account, and that there are platforms for the voices of adults who are care experienced, has grown. This is not the case for young people within the criminal justice system and, should they intersect with also being a child in care, they are less likely to be among those who are invited to, or would seek out to attend 'participation' settings. This is even less so for those working within the system with a criminal justice background whose silence might be fuelled by shame around those experiences, fear of upsetting the employer or concerns about blurring professional boundaries.

This intersectional lens offers insights that are often left unarticulated yet Brierley not only contextually articulates his experiences, but seeks to provide a new framework through which youth justice can effect change.

Times have changed and the model of 'mad,' 'bad' or 'sad' is outdated and ignores the extensive evidence, research and wisdom that we have to hand. The real question then has to be, will we choose to use it? Will we be committed to going deeply within ourselves to harness an empathy that can truly create and shape relationships that make the difference.

A system that incarcerates, isolates and punishes the individual is not a system that recognises relational wealth as the primary resource because, if it did, we would wrap high quality relationships around all the children and young people who need it. The time for change is 'now,' It has always been 'now' and it will always be 'now.' Allow Brierley to walk alongside you on this journey of curiosity, connection and compassion.

Lisa Cherry, January 2021

Lisa Cherry is an author, trainer and speaker on Trauma, Recovery and Resilience. She brings 30 years of experience working in education and social care settings which, in the last ten years, through delivering training across all sectors, has expanded to include criminal justice and health. Her research in her Masters in Education looked at the intersection of school exclusion and being in care, and the impact upon education and employment across the life course. She is currently undertaking her PhD at Oxford University to continue this research.

Lisa Cherry brings together academic research, professional experience and personal stories creating a holistic approach to working with vulnerability, with a fundamental belief that with the right relationships we have the capacity to recover.

CHAPTER 1

The Who, the Why and the Context

This is a journey that will explore how society or services communicate, engage or connect with children, teenagers and young people that are caught up in our youth justice system, especially those whose conduct is serious or persistent. Those that are most at risk of being involved in gangs, criminal exploitation, drug addiction, county lines, as we will find, inevitably make up a large proportion of the inmates that reside in our very expensive prison system. These young people often find themselves excluded from social and educational norms early in their development or life trajectory. For instance, a UK Parliament report, 'Education in Youth Custody' (2016) found that,

> 'around 90 per cent of children in custody had been excluded from school at any one point before entering custody and 63 per cent of boys had been permanently excluded and 74 per cent of girls.'

There is a bit of a chicken and egg question in the education sector about correlation or causation. There seems to be a pipeline from educational exclusion to prison which we will explore in more detail.

Almost all of these children will have had some involvement with either early help, prevention services, alternative educational provision or children's social work services. So then why, if we often know who they are and provide services for them so early in their life course, are we unable to modify their behaviour or life trajectory? Is the implication that their poor life outcomes are their own fault and simply a matter of poor choices? Is it that the services that claim to effect change in this group have limitations to their effectiveness? Are we attempting to change children when it is their environment that needs to change because, after all, children are a response to their environment?

This book will take you on a journey and explore these and other questions in greater detail. In *Chapter 5*, 'The Risk Switch' we will explore what I believe is my unique perspective on youth justice and how justice practitioners overcome barriers to engagement caused by viewing matters via an implicit bias lens. Society overtly judges those that offend so does that apply to justice practitioners? Are they exempt from that judgement and, if not, does that impact on relationships between the two? Are relationships even important in a justice context when trying to change behaviour, particularly young people's behaviour?

My own journey

After experiencing a childhood riddled with adversity, instability and toxic stress, I behaved in ways as a young person that society defined as deviant, anti-social and criminal. I used various substances to help me manage my emotional dysregulation, distress and social rejection which left a feeling of pain that I tried to hide away from. These factors led to my cognitive impairments, the inability to learn new things or concentrate, which inevitably affected my daily decision-making (US Department of Health and Human Services, 2011).

With hindsight and reflection as an adult, these now seem, to me at least, to be an adaptation to my childhood relationships and certainly contributed to my poor life choices. As a child my environmental choices were made for me. When being worked with by teachers, police officers, judges, youth workers, prison or probation officers, getting me to take responsibility for my behaviour and actions was their primary objective. Their focus on changing my behaviour was at times a barrier to building a relationship based on trust. This was often ineffective in the absence of such a relationship and, at 17, I was incarcerated (an experience that was re-traumatising) after I was coerced into selling drugs by adults.

My childhood experiences left me vulnerable to child criminal exploitation and eventually I experienced four prison sentences as a young person which all related to substance misuse, including heroin addiction. Various chapters in this book will ask questions about how we can work together with communities to prevent children being exploited into crime, including the interface between justice systems or authority and poor, disadvantaged communities. At whether we are able to prevent those exploited young people passing this unfortunate experience onto others, both as peers and as parents, which is often described as the intergenerational cycle of abuse. I have invited young adults with direct experience of being recipients of the youth justice system to offer their insights. They have experience of working with me directly, which will offer qualitative experience from a practical level of young people (now adults) I have worked with over the years who have experienced youth justice. They will also discuss their views of how criminal identities develop and what we as justice professionals can do to help avoid this.

My transition has been from prisoner to youth justice specialist and in my first book *Your Honour Can I Tell You My Story?* I disclosed many examples of programme development and relationship building with the most serious and prolific young people in trouble. This new book aims to join the personal with the professional. As I developed the ability to appropriately reflect and articulate the challenges faced by children that are incarcerated, I felt sharing my story could help others better understand how we as young people in trouble get there. Stories matter and they can help society empathise with children such as I was when they come into conflict with the law and create victims, often after being victims themselves. My first book has also I think been successful in simultaneously offering other incarcerated young people a practical example of how I navigated my way through the labels applied by society and the justice system and not being defined by them. How I overcame my own poor decision-making and relational experiences that continually held me back.

Fresh insights as a professional

Since joining youth justice as a professional, I have advanced my knowledge of child development, behavioural responses to trauma and the justice system itself. Although children like I was make poor choices which can at times cause harm to others, this tends to be a response to bio-psychosocial factors. As we will explore in *Chapter 7*, 'Youth Crime and Trauma,' a child developing through adversity or exposure to harm experiences toxic stress and this can damage their developing brain. Many are describing this now as 'developmental trauma' due in part to the work of leading psychiatrists such as Bessel Van Der Kolk (2015) in the medical, neurobiological, academic and children's services world.

We will look outside the justice system to these fields to explore what contributes to identity formation, specifically of a criminal identity. All these factors have shaped my perspective and practice. However as I am not a professor, doctor or academic I will explore these matters and discuss them in a language that I hope is accessible to everyone at all levels of their professional development and will stay focused on youth crime.

This journey will steer us through relational experiences and human connections built on trust within the youth justice system, which offer special insights; navigating professional and lived experiences and also exploring the work of experts, such as Dan Siegel's *Interpersonal Neurobiology* (2015) and Felitti et al's 'Adverse Childhood Experiences Study' (1998) amongst others:

- deep diving into the environmental and relational challenges of children and young people that develop criminal identities and looking at how their identities are often constructed though their relational experiences as they develop;
- exploring how inequality impacts on them throughout childhood and asking whether the justice system or services shaped to improve their life circumstances improve equity, or create yet more adversity for the child or family to navigate; and together
- we will consider key components to building relationships with young people in trouble, knowing this has helped me achieve engagement, connection and understanding.

Exploring childhood trauma and adverse childhood experiences in *Chapter 7*, I will introduce the 'ACEs & Social Inequality Window.' This is a visual model that demonstrates how relational poverty and economic instability impact on children experiencing structural inequality and presents stressful events to the very young people with the least resources to appropriately manage stress. I will demonstrate and highlight that young people in trouble are often adapting to or surviving their relational environments, rather than lacking resilience (which is often the view of those that have not had these experiences).

We will also examine whether there is a link between childhood developmental trauma, ACEs and youth crime. This is of course a follow-up of my first book to explore why we seemingly have least success in modifying the behaviour of teenagers like myself described as 'hard to reach,' 'disengaged,' 'challenging,' 'aggressive,' or 'dysregulated,' within the criminal justice and care systems. Does attachment and trauma impact on relationship building and, if it does, how do we address that in a justice context? Sharing my experiences as a professional, building trusting relationships with young people in trouble and also my lived experience as a traumatised young person in the youth justice and prison systems for almost a decade, we will also explore the literature and the connection or relationship between trauma and youth crime.

Your Honour Can I Tell You My Story? explored the benefits of *lived experience* of involvement with criminal justice and how this 'shared' social experience can help when building rapport with young people in trouble. Those with lived experience of navigating justice services or being risk-assessed who have modified their own life trajectories are in a unique position to reach in and mentor this group. We will examine why I believe this is the case in *Chapter 6*, 'Joint Enterprise.' I will share how lived experience helps, how it offers the component of connection due to common identity, how we can all gain from this if we are open to learning from those we aim to help. Lived experience can help in relationship building but there are other key components that are just as essential. Our journey will include exploring literature and the lived experience perspective, combining key ingredients of a harmonious feast; one which brings both sides of the justice fence to the table.

When it comes to youth crime, we immediately look at engagement in education, reducing drug use or introducing positive activities in young people's intervention plans which are often created through assessment. These often-external factors are important and address some of the symptoms of youth crime; however, we must consider whether they address the root causes. We will concentrate on the relational experiences young people in trouble have and how we can seek to better understand and connect with them and reduce barriers to relationship building. If we only try to modify the external factors the young person relies upon to navigate their adversity, they may be unlikely to view us as the relational buffer they require for behavioural change. If they view us as a risk, or people that may cause harm, or if we are not relationally available, they will likely 'disengage,' so we will concentrate on that complexity.

In *Chapter 5*, I introduce the 'Risk Switch' model which is a visual example of what can happen when young people transition from being vulnerable children to becoming perpetrators, exploiters, offenders and criminals through the service lens. How this often takes place before their brain has fully developed and matured and what the social impact of this can be within their communities, and also with their younger peers and relational networks. The intricate complexity this Risk Switch can have with child criminal exploitation and whether this contributes to young people and adults calling services a 'system.' The Risk Switch also offers justice practitioners a visual reminder to hold the child service recipient born into challenging circumstances at the heart of any intervention or plan as they grow. Stressing the importance of this within a justice context through a relational lens. Attachment and adversity, as we will find, lasts a lifetime, so is it important to think about the relational experience of the developing child, even when they are at adolescence or are young adults when they commit crime?

We often discuss lived experience and co-production which at times becomes tokenistic consultation with service recipients or young people. However, those of us with similar backgrounds of developmental trauma and those who were privileged enough not to have experienced such trauma, or had relational buffers to reduce impact, should share our knowledge and experience and work together for the best outcomes for all children. Having lived on both sides of the criminal justice fence, I believe everyone has different expertise and, together, we can really make a difference to children's lives. We just have to be open-minded enough to learn from each other and respect each others' journeys and our adaptations to them. We all bring something to the table in terms of diverse views and opinions.

Professionals working in youth justice services often try their best and yet find it challenging to effect change with this group of young people in trouble. We will explore this complexity in *Chapter 4* 'A Unique Perspective of Relational Justice' and how we can focus on improving relationship building. What are the experiences these young people have had that make them avoid services that are trying to support them? Why do they place themselves in what we perceive to be risky situations and relationships?

A 'Beyond Youth Custody' report (Bateman, 2013) found that over two thirds of young people under 18 reoffend within 12 months of release from secure institutions. This group is 50 per cent made up of children that have spent time in care, while overall only one per cent of UK children are in care at any one time (Laming, 2016); while 45 per cent are from black or minority ethnic (BAME) backgrounds, despite them making up only 18 per cent of the ten-to-17-year-old population (Cooper, 2019). I myself was care experienced and also reoffended within 12 months of release from youth custody. However, I truly believe that, with the right relational experiences and support, these statistics need not be an inevitability.

We do however also have to consider relationships and the way they play on this group becoming excluded, and also how relationships play a role in making sure they are included, which will reduce youth crime as a result. We will explore what it means to be a 'trauma-informed' justice professional. Complete a deep dive into the world in which many of the young people live as better understanding their experience can only be beneficial to relationship building.

It is a journey that will question what services believe the barriers are to turning this group's behaviour around and why that perspective was different for many I grew up with within the justice system. It is that interesting complexity that has driven me to write this book. We have to be able to bridge that disconnect in some way for us to truly make a difference on a societal level. Social marginalisation exists, so are we improving these young people's life opportunities or adding to their social challenges? These are questions we can ask throughout this journey and examine the answers from a multi-dimensional perspective. I certainly don't hold all the answers, however I believe I have a valuable insight into relationships within justice settings. My professional title includes the word 'Specialist'; however, I am not writing this book because I think I have all the strategic answers. It is clear to me that the answer only lies in one place, and that is in relationships and human connections. Everything else, including processes, strategy and culture is secondary. I also believe I have extensive knowledge and skills of relationship building with this particular group. I have done it in one context or another all my life and, as a result of this track record, this is where I think my specialism lies.

I intend to draw out as many questions of the system itself as I can possibly provide answers. I would describe myself as an *expert witness* of relationship building with young people in trouble. As I have already said, I have spent a lifetime connecting with them from both sides of the justice fence. I have navigated countless traumatised relationships and four prison sentences as I mentioned above, spanning over four years. This instilled a natural ability to communicate, connect and engage with people of all ages within the prison system. I have then used these skills to also navigate a professional career in youth justice and wanted to share how these experiences have shaped my relational practice and interconnected approaches with others. I will explain why I believe, with the best will in the world, that the system itself is part of the solution, and at times also part of the problem. The best justice practitioners are reflective enough to understand that intricate dynamic. They view things through the lens of the recipient; using their connection gained through relationships to reduce the likelihood of further harmful behaviour, as the vehicle to effective practice.

I hope the following insights from this multi-dimensional perspective of literature, service recipient and service provider can go some way to helping justice workers, police officers, social workers, prison officers, judges and other professionals to find that relational space with service recipients which is 'where the magic happens.' Relationships are a reciprocal process, so obtaining 'buy-in' from young people in trouble is the only road to improved life outcomes for those with behavioural problems. If we don't, we will continue to see poor outcomes and high recidivism for some of our most prolific but also vulnerable children as they develop: through the Risk Switch I will describe. It is in our best interests to obtain positive outcomes for them socially, financially and morally. Your political allegiances or belief in punishment or rehabilitation shouldn't matter. We all want less victims and improved life trajectories for this marginalised group, whilst simultaneously safeguarding the most vulnerable children and creating better communities for us all to live in.

After all, relationships are the conduit to change and, without them, the young people will refuse to become receptive of the support we provide. In the words of Maya Angelou,

> 'Children often won't remember what you say, or what you did, they will likely remember how you made them feel.'

In the final chapter, after taking a journey through the complex experiences of many of these young people and the relationships they have with the system itself, I will share the key components of building empathetic and secure attachments with young people and adolescents that do not trust professionals for various reasons. It is possible, it just takes understanding and sometimes recognising the intricate complexities of your position in the young person's life and what you need to do to become a significant part of it. I hold the strong belief that the only way to significantly change a young person's behaviour is to be a significant relationship in that young person's life.

CHAPTER 2

It Takes a Village to Raise a Child

Children of doctors are 24 times more likely than their peers to become doctors. Children of lawyers are 17 times more likely to go into law, and children of those in film or television are 12 times more likely to enter these fields. The same pattern is repeated in architecture and in certain of the arts. These findings are set out in a book entitled *The Class Ceiling: Why it Pays to be Privileged* (2019) by Sam Friedman, a professor at the London School of Economics, and Daniel Laurison, Assistant Professor of Sociology at Swarthmore College. They demonstrate that opportunity is provided by the hands of those in positions of privilege through networks of relationships, family support and encouragement. Nothing new in that, I hear you say, and why shouldn't families help their children to become successful. In short, there is nothing wrong with it.

This just highlights that family networks provide opportunities for children to be successful. As a result, they are significantly more likely to follow in their parents' footsteps and life choices. Although, I am sure most of these parents feel there are often significant differences in characteristics, temperament or behaviours between them and their children, the children clearly have their life choices significantly influenced by their parents' choices.

Relational poverty

For children growing-up in challenging households characterised by violence, criminality, substance misuse and unemployment, their ability to *not* follow in their parents' footsteps becomes far more limited due to social marginalisation and exclusion. This is relational poverty (Perry, 2011; Lawson et al, 2018) which we will explore throughout this journey. In his book *Born to Love: Why Empathy is Essential and Endangered,* Bruce Perry (Ibid) describes a form of poverty that impacts us all, regardless of race, gender, age, or socio-economic status. Perry's 'relational poverty' is just what it sounds like; a deep lack of the connectedness with others that we all need to survive and in order to be well. It also implies a theory or theories of causality. Lawson states that,

> 'in contrast to prevalent understanding that root economic hardship in the deficits of individuals or families or subcultures, the theory asserts that poverty is best explained by patterns of human relationships.'

Relational poverty is not defined by socio-economic circumstances as much as it is by intergenerational trauma or familial cycles of abuse. A study by Widom (1989) found that one in six maltreated boys and girls go on to become violent offenders. This is incredibly high given most children never come into contact with the youth justice system at all, let alone for violent offences. Children can grow-up in economic hardship and receive nurturing relationships during childhood and adolescence. However, if a child grows up faced with the adversities that tend to sit alongside economic hardship and is not provided with nurturing relationships due to the relational networks being characterised by trauma, criminality and violence, this is relational poverty. My own childhood was entrenched in both. The relational poverty was far more harmful and yes it was compounded by the lack of financial stability, albeit they often intertwined like the branches of a thorn bush.

Life is full of choices for children; however, the family we are born into or the 'village' we develop in is never a choice. The question is, for children involved in serious or prolific offending, how much choice have they had about the shaping of their identity and how much does this contribute to the choices they make? Being born into a family that is characterised by factors that mean other families in the village avoid them is certainly not a choice made by a child within the said family. Consider the child growing-up in a family that develops a criminal identity through criminal relational connections and networks. It is logical that they are far more likely, due to having a lack of supportive relational networks, to follow in their parents' footsteps than those families listed at the start of this chapter. Certainly, they are more likely to develop a similar identity because they are exposed to far fewer relationships offering alternative identities through the relational experience.

Offending, relationships and identity

Let's take a moment to explore the connection between offending, relationships and identity. The first port of call is to explore what the justice system thinks about the connection. *Desistance* is one of the more enduring modern theories that underpin the criminal justice system (McNeill, 2012). The definitions remain contested by researchers, however most think of desistance as a process of changing criminal behaviour. This process is broken down into 'primary' desistance, which refers to the absence of offending behaviour for any period in time. However, this is distinct from 'secondary' desistance, which refers to a much more deep-seated change in the person, reflected in their developing an *identity* and perception of themselves as a non-offender (Clinks, 2013).

In principle, I fully agree with the desistance theory as desistance effectively means people involved in offending do not have an epiphany or moment of realisation when it comes to desisting from crime. Crime, in any case, is a social construct, which is adopted by the inhabitants of a society to signify incidents that break the law. Until the Sexual Offences Act 1967, being homosexual was illegal in the UK, something constructed by its inhabitants. This highlights that crimes can vary from one country to the next. The concept of breaking the law can also vary from one decade to the next and what feels morally right or wrong now may be challenged in the future. In retrospect, we could be viewed as immoral for constructing such laws. One day, we may look back and wonder how or why we criminalised disadvantaged and traumatised children at the age of ten in England and Wales. Or maybe not and I am just drawing on my unconscious bias which I of course have on issues around crime and children (of which I am not ashamed because if we get it right with children who offend there will be less victims).

People of all ages commit crimes on one particular day and then, due to a lack of opportunity or drive, never do so again. Lots of people certainly will not view themselves as offenders when buying a stolen TV or iPhone from someone in their local community. This is especially true when it comes to items stolen from commercial organizations. This is seen as 'justification' due to viewing big business as an acceptable victim, in my experience, and people often disassociate from the crime because the victim is an entity rather than a person. I have witnessed some disadvantaged folk believe they are often excluded from obtaining certain consumer goods and believe methods of this kind are the only way they can obtain them. It is my observation that the law impacts on different people in different ways and, if you're poor, isolated, marginalised or economically disadvantaged, the law often impacts on you more than if you are wealthy or even just economically stable.

There are those within society that commit crime regularly and rarely get caught because they are functional and organized and better at breaking the rules. This very rarely applies to those young people who come into contact with the youth justice system. Most of those that find their way into the more punitive stages of the system such as those in young offender institutions, I will argue, have been shaped by their relational experiences within their village. These relationships have either exposed them to criminal identities within their families and communities, or else they have sought out relational protection due to feeling unsafe for one reason or another. As a result, they may have found attachments at home or elsewhere in their community that they perceive keep them safe or provide some hope or sense of belonging. In this instance, it's relationships that are interconnected through shared identity and shared experiences that create group membership. In *Chapter 5*, 'The Risk Switch,' we will explore how this impacts on child criminal exploitation.

The criminal justice system spends billions of pounds every year trying to change the identity of thousands of people that enter the justice system. Therefore, I am amazed that there is very little research to be found on how young people develop criminal identities in the first place. There have been various links made between prison and school exclusion and even the care system (Laming, 2016; Lochner,2004). These links have been challenged by the education and the care sectors as correlations but not causations. They are of course correct. Drug use, exploitation itself and exposure to criminality are all correlating factors which contribute to developing an identity, but not a cause of youth crime. This, as we will find, is more often than not the same for school exclusion and also the care experience.

However, if the principal aim of the justice system is to change the *criminal identities* of those who offend, the system itself has to recognise identity to be one of the most significant factors. So then, where on earth are all these children developing a criminal identity from? Also, if we know the families they are most likely to come from, should not early intervention and educating the 'village' at a child's developmental stages be the focus of the youth justice system? Working with the villagers would seem to be a more effective and productive way of tackling youth crime than changing teenagers' identities. Anyone parenting a teenager knows that trying to change their behaviour can be extremely challenging. Even just trying to get them to clean their rooms or do their homework, so what are the chances of changing their identity? Wow, now that would take some assessment or programme content, don't you think?

Dr Dan Siegal in his book *The Developing Mind* (2nd edn, 2015) explains that 'our relational connections shape our neural connections.' This means the relationships that surround a child help to develop their brain's function and structure, together with their mind and how they view themselves and the world as they grow. Albeit, Siegal also explains that our genes form part of our temperament and other areas of character, even epigenetics is shaped by our experiences of relationships and social environment, which is inevitably the child's village. This certainly helps explain the 'following in the parents' footsteps' of Sam Friedman's *The Class Ceiling*. Yet, when a child reaches a court-room for a crime, which is often a moment in their lifetime of challenges, the narrative presented by the village press is that they are 'thugs' and 'criminals' simply making choices. Seems a little unjust and excluding to me, to blame the child for responding to a relational village environment they played no role in creating. The childhood of being a victim is not as important as a moment of being an offender.

I have a four-year-old daughter now and I am more convinced than ever that Siegal is absolutely right. She simply mimics my behaviour towards her because she knows little else. She dresses her dolls for school and plays the role of the teacher and even enjoys taking the dolls to the toilet as we do with her. We are in the midst of a worldwide pandemic as I write this chapter and playing families with her in her bedroom yesterday she told me she was 'working from home,' replicating her mother's current work circumstances and behaviours. She is developing a sense of who she is by observing her parents' behaviour towards her. She is developing a sense of self, identity and perspective through her environment and relationships. This is not a conscious, thinking process; it is a natural and organic part of her development through attachment rela-tionships. For me, it highlights relational disparity from my fatherless home and a mother who was an isolated 17-year-old care leaver when I was born, surrounding herself with other adults, dealing with unmet needs and in the midst of criminal and addictive behaviours. The process is largely down to what we call 'mirror neurons.' It really uncovered for me my childhood exposure to instability, abuse, neglect and, more importantly for this book, what I call relational criminality developing my identity, that the justice system spent so many years trying to change.

Mirror neurons have been suggested to 'play a role in not only understanding the actions of others, but perhaps even their intentions' (Kolb and Whishaw, 2009, p. 82). Leading experts in experiential learning are excited by the discovery of mirror neurons. They believe this 'creates the opportunity for a baby to not only imitate their parents, but also to learn the action.' In that way they gain experience in how to move their mouth and tongue and how to connect with their parents. This imitation, even though not fully conscious, is not a reflex (Morban and Cruz, 2016). This explains my daughter's behaviours mirroring mine, but more importantly, for youth crime, me mirroring years of exposure to adults involved in criminal behaviour, violence and drug use. Hence my gravitation towards others with similar identities and behaviours and them becoming my in-group. How is a young person to assess a potential perpetrator of exploitation if they have been raised by those with the exact same behaviours and characteristics? The adult that exploited me as a young person was not a risk to me, he was a familiar and safe relationship as a result of my adaptations to my own reality.

We are also aware that mirror neurons are largely responsible for developing culture and language. We now understand 'similar mirror neurons in the language regions of the frontal cortex are likely responsible for the mimicking of sounds and words by children' (Kolb and Whishaw, 2009, p. 534). My wife is Spanish and our daughter is bilingual. People often say she is clever for speaking two languages at four-years-of-age. I am not suggesting she isn't clever, however speaking Spanish is not an indicator of intelligence, simply because it is taking place through the natural developmental process via mirror neurons. I am still not able to speak Spanish anywhere near her level. Anyone that has tried to speak a second language after the age of 30 will probably empathise with me. She is far more advanced and that makes me feel great as you can imagine but it is not because she is more intelligent than I am. It is simply that she is inculcated in a language at a stage when her mirror neurons are receptive to developing rapidly through environment and relationships.

This explains why, as I experienced, prisoners develop their own language and culture, and I know why I adapted to that culture to fit in and feel safe in an unsafe environment. Dan Siegal feels that mirror neurons should be called 'sponge neurons' because they act as a sponge when children are developing and therefore shape their identity and self-perception, and even language. I find this most interesting given we spend billions changing that identity when youngsters make poor choices and enter youth justice or become adult offenders, grounded in the desistance theory as I have already explained. Even that the press publicly demonises them when they make poor choices, which have often been significantly shaped by their environment and relationships.

In all my years on both sides of the justice system, young people have often been seen as rational actors with a few predispositions, social determinants or risk factors that correlate to youth crime. Ultimately, we do little about the relational factors that shape children's identities, but try with our might and will to change the child. How must this feel for a child who doesn't have the capacity to understand the shaping of their identity and how this links to their behaviour? They will always seek to protect their carers because parental attachment requires them to do so to survive. They may often feel they are forced to choose between their attachment figures and authority figures, of which there will only be one winner. Yes, they say it takes a village to raise a child, but this conflicting existence is unlikely to feel like a caring village life viewed through the child's lens.

On a personal level, I always understood that my mum loved me. However, because her own childhood had been shaped by experiences of neglect and abuse, she didn't 'see' me the way a small child needs to be seen. She didn't have a good enough blueprint of relationships to be able to parent me safely, or meet my emotional, educational or safety needs; and the services, although involved, were unable to help her develop the capacity do so. The absence of any father figure and living with a traumatised teenage mum inevitably impacted my development and critically my identity formation. My mother's position within society, her self-worth and self-perception, all contributed to her ability or otherwise to access positive relationships. However and just like anyone else, as a woman with unmet needs she sought attachments which often came in the form of abusive relationships with men who also had unmet needs.

Being raised by an abused teenager who hadn't had the relational experience to heal from her own experiences of abuse brought with it consequences for me and my siblings as children which stayed with us into adulthood. Mum struggled to assess risk in others, had limited access to positive male relationships and yet needed to be loved by men; this exposed my developing brain to relational harm. Instability, neglect, abuse, violence, poor role models, a lack of education, substance misuse and significantly relational criminality all shaped my neural connections and sense of who I was and where I fitted into the world. However, most importantly, this exposure to what we now know as toxic stress (Shonkoff et al, 2012) and chronic developmental trauma (Van Der Kolk, 2015) happened in the context of my village. Much easier to be inducted into Spanish to be honest.

Dr Siegal, in his talk 'How Relationships Shape Us' (2017) articulates far better than I can that children develop their sense of identity by understanding their village companions. He explains that 'children understand the attention, intention and awareness of others which shapes their own neural machinery, even before they understand that they have a conscious mind.' He also explains that humans have evolved over millions of years and we are the only mammals that have done so by sharing our responsibility of parenting with non-birth parents, or 'alloparenting' (care provided by non-parents). Growing-up in my household pre and post the care experience due to abuse and neglect, my mother alloparented me with various adults involved in violence and criminality. Therefore, although I of course made choices, as do all children that end up in custody, the identity that the justice system would later punish me into changing was outside my control. Dr Siegal also explains that, 'Your very capacity for consciousness and self-awareness is relational.' This concept was never discussed in my decade of youth justice interventions. I was just told I was often 'led' by my peers into offending but we never explored why I was always drawn towards and comfortable in relationships that caused me harm.

Those relationships played a role in not only shaping my identity, but also led me to those I felt were 'my kind of people,' or my in-group. If mirror neurons are responsible for anything, it is how we start to shape our behaviour, connections and attachments. This explains my daughter behaving in the way she observes her parents behaving. Therefore, it's not only the negative relationships themselves that create a sense of identity, but as well as this the lack of supportive, attuned relationships that can offer some level of protection to a developing child. This also offers some response to the argument that many put forward when they say, 'I grew up in a rough area and I didn't commit crime or become addicted to drugs.' Identity, as we have found, starts to develop way before a child reaches school or is conscious about its behaviour. It's often because of access to safe adult relationships that support an identity developing, way before they come into contact with any potentially negative relationships out in their communities. This is a relational *privilege* that we don't discuss enough, that we will dive into further in *Chapter 7*, when exploring 'Youth Crime and Trauma.'

'But we have children's social work services to support families when they are struggling in the village,' I hear you say. Services including early help and family support often respond to families that are vulnerable and to safeguarding concerns. This doesn't always include offending within the family or wider networks. The children of a father who is sent to prison for organized crime, e.g. wouldn't automatically come to the attention of support services, unless there was a safeguarding concern due to those children being left with their mother or other family members. Protection from the creation of such an identity has to come from supportive relationships within the village, however the villagers residing in such areas have enough on their hands protecting their children from community harm. Therefore, it seems society has been designed in a way that leaves the most vulnerable exposed to the most harm. The subjective perception passed on generationally through this group is that authority takes *their* children into care and places *their* people in custody. This, in my view, explains the fear of authority which feeds into the exploitation of children and high reoffending rates post-custody (Prison Reform Trust, 2019).

Offending is a behaviour and if children see adults justify crime it is likely to shape that child's view of offending behaviour and authority. It is not just a case of choices based on values and beliefs, which is the perception of many professionals within the justice system. Programmes have been tailored towards helping change the belief system that young people in trouble have that offending is socially acceptable. However, it is rooted in their relational experiences. In fact they often believe offending to be unacceptable but participate in it to maintain attachments to relationships they feel comfortable and safe within in their perceived unsafe world. Also, even when social care is involved, it doesn't mean they believe their work is to prevent exposure to petty crime or the behaviours of community members involved in criminal activity *per se*. It is primarily to safeguard the child through child protection measures.

The following paragraph is an extract from my care files after I was returned home from foster care due to emotional, sexual and physical abuse and harm; social care was seemingly aware I was returned to be exposed to relational criminality, and yet shortly after that they closed the case. The reality of toxic stress and childhood adversity for those young people caught up in the justice system is cumulative in nature and almost impossible to explain in adolescence. Despite this knowledge, I can find no evidence of any intervention with mum or adults in the home, or support to explore how this would affect me as a developing child at that point or in my future. It might not have been effective, or ultimately changed my outcome, but is that a reason not to at least speak to adults about their behaviour and its impact and record this? Should this have followed me to the justice system, because it seems important given what we are finding out about identity formation and even desistance?

> 'He seems intimately familiar with who was who's boyfriend, (amongst the adults) who had fallen out and who was in trouble with the police. He obviously picks up all the gossip as before, with little filters.
>
> However he seems to be coping at home and at school.'

People who commit crime in areas of deprivation are not always viewed negatively by people within their communities. Villagers don't always know the details of others' offending behaviour, only that they offend. If villagers are themselves struggling through poverty and structural inequity, they are likely to at least empathise with those who bend the rules more than those society works for. This doesn't mean everyone living in poverty is offending, just that they often have to navigate relationships with those that do offend. This poses a risk to children like me growing-up, by implying that everyone in the village offends in some way, even though that is not true. I have found this resonates with many of the children I have worked with. Even when challenged, they often refuse to accept that most people do not offend. I believe the reason for this is that it is their subjective reality, i.e. that most people do offend. Similarly, I asked a child that was excluded from school what percentage of children he felt do not complete school. He replied, 'Fifty percent.' This told me everything I needed to know about his subjective reality and truth.

Attachment, authenticity and other crossovers

There is a crossover between factors that lead children into support services and those that lead them into offending as stated by the Youth Justice Board (2016) in their response to Lord Laming's 'Review of the Care System' (2016). However, if we accept as a society that, if a child is heavily involved in offending, their identity has been shaped by their relational experiences, we may start to ask more questions about their environment during development than we do about their behaviour.

We often talk about trauma responsive institutions; but this is how a trauma responsive village would look to me. A village that:

- assembles its whole infrastructure on the wellbeing of children;
- fundamentally embraces the idea that children need protecting from poverty, inequality and harm; and
- embraces the idea that, to have better communities, we need to develop better brains in all children by looking after vulnerable parents.

Instead we have assembled one that pays taxes for the state to improve children's resilience to tackle the adversity the adults in the village have created.

We have witnessed first-hand the response to the Covid-19 crisis because it is a common problem for all and affects every family regardless of colour, class or status (albeit even Covid-19 harms certain groups more than others). If we had a village that was willing to adjust itself in a similar way to prevent harm coming to children in the way we have responded to Covid-19, it would reduce crime, poor mental health, pressure on the NHS, homelessness and drugs and alcohol abuse, which I will return to in *Chapter 8*. It is a common social problem, not just a problem for the disadvantaged, so it requires the same level of social adjustment, commitment and belief that we are all responsible. If we continue to blame the disadvantaged for being disadvantaged, we are simply missing the fact that their decisions don't cause poverty, they are often a symptom of poverty. Relationships are central to wellbeing and poverty places a strain on relationships. If children are raised by adults exposed to intersectionality (overlapping and interdependent forms of disadvantage, etc.), intergenerational trauma, poverty and structural inequality, they are less likely to receive the supportive, nurturing relationships for them to develop self-worth and a sense of belonging to the village.

Children often show us their developmental experiences within their villages through their behaviour as they grow. They demonstrate, as I did, what their relational experience has been when they reach an age when their behaviour becomes criminal, anti-social or just 'naughty.' They often don't remember, can't articulate or simply don't understand the link between their relational experience and behaviour. This is often due to lack of maturity or capacity and frequently the fact that their trauma may have happened before they could talk. If developmental trauma plays a role in their behavioural issues, this is simply not their fault. Research indicates that the average age of first memory is around three-and-half-years-old. If many of us cannot remember what happened in our childhoods before we reached school, how can they?

Dr Gabor Mate, who is an expert in the field of attachment and addiction, states in his talk 'The Need for Authenticity' (Mate, 2016) that children can grow-up in households where they have to sacrifice their *authenticity* for their *attachments*. Authenticity is the ability to reflect and understand one's self and to express how one feels. Attachment is love, care and attention from an adult, primarily a parent or carer who can care for and protect you. Both are a human need; however, attachment is the most essential need as it is how we survive as infants. Children will always ensure their attachment needs are met for that reason. We often say children exploited into crime have attachment issues and children looked after are often the children at most risk (Children's Society, 2018). An obvious question for me having been through this process is, 'Why do these children attach to exploiters and not professionals trying to help? Can we continue to avoid questions of how we operate as children's services which can scare or alienate vulnerable children and families, rather than connect with them and keep them safe?' If we do not get the response to this right in a measured and less authoritarian way, we may make things worse in the long-term.

Without attachment as humans we will die because we are solely dependent on our carers as infants and are the most vulnerable of all mammals at birth. Often, children have to give up their authenticity to maintain a relationship with their parents and other adults and to maintain their attachments. Then we often claim that they are emotionally illiterate when they enter youth justice. However, they have learnt strategies to cope without expressing how they feel, to survive the unsafe world they perceive they live in. Expressing their emotions may leave them more vulnerable or rejected and this is when toxic masculinity (UKessays, 2018) appears. This often means they arrive at adulthood with no sense of who they are emotionally, which often results in addiction or other poor outcomes such as violent crime and the horrendous cycle of domestic violence. In the words of Dr Gabor Mate (2009),

'Not everyone that is traumatized becomes addicted, but everyone that is addicted was traumatized.'

In my experience, most of my group when I was a teenage heroin addict were children excluded from school and/or those in care. Others tried heroin but didn't fall into addiction the way we vulnerable children did, so Gabor is likely correct about who gets addicted, not everyone that uses recreationally.

I've been working with young boys in youth justice over the past decade, they often use the term 'my boys' when describing their peers. They explain that their boys will always have their back and often commit themselves fully to the cause of their group. This is often a telltale sign that they perceive the world to be an unsafe place and are seeking attachments to maintain safety which is a basic human need. We wouldn't have lasted very long in evolutionary times if we hadn't used what we had at our disposal to maintain safety, now would we? These children do not view the village authority as a protective factor to save them from harm. They seek protection elsewhere in the village through their relational network, using both their initiative and resources which has all been shaped by their previous relational experiences. Professor Brene Brown explains 'If you trade your authenticity for safety, you may experience the following: anxiety, depression, eating disorders, addiction, rage, blame, resentment, and inexplicable grief.' We seem to be providing a perfect storm for vulnerable boys to hide who they are to survive and then punishing them for their resilience.

We are developing our knowledge of children that enter the youth justice system and of the exploitation process, however I am not sure adapting the current system is the right response. Is this a 'trauma-responsive' system, now we know about biological adaptation to growing-up in a village filled with relational harm? We must focus on changing the village rather than the child if we are to improve outcomes and develop more cost-effective services with reduced recidivism. During my time as a so-called 'criminal,' no-one ever showed an interest in my relationships as I grew. No-one ever mentioned to me that developmental trauma could have played a role in my behaviour, which contributed to my offending. The point I make here isn't to say that if that had been said or understood, it I would have stopped me from offending or I would have desisted. It is that the experts are telling us loud and clear about the why, so we should not compound their criminal identities with harmful responses to circumstances they have little control over.

The following paragraph from a pre-sentence report describes my early years. It was written and submitted by probation when I was 20-years-old and standing before a judge before sentencing.

'OFFENDER ASSESSMENT

Andrew Brierley says he has had a fairly disruptive childhood. His parents separated when he was very young and his mother moved many times. He is the eldest of five children and due to his sister being abused, spent time in care for a while. He was expelled from school at the age of fifteen without qualifications but states he has no literacy or numeracy problems. At this time, he began associating with people who introduced him to drugs and he says he tried any and every drug available including heroin.'

Somewhere along the line we have become obsessed with the idea that, when it comes to youth crime, there is a perpetrator and a victim. We have lost sight of the fact that children who experience exposure to relational criminality that shapes their identity are victims themselves. No child is born with the desire to be excluded from school, addicted to drugs or sent to prison and, if this happens, they are victims of their own circumstances as well as perpetrators of any crime they commit. Maybe if we recognised this, the age of criminal responsibility would not be as low as ten and generations of children may not have been exploited under our supervision. For decades, we have been saying things like, 'This is what the latest research tells us' when our children have been sexually and criminally exploited, yet we have needed serious case reviews to make us aware of the extent of this. This tells us there is something wrong relationally with how we provide services to the disadvantaged. Why do we need serious case reviews or further research to find out our children are being exploited or abused *en masse*? What else haven't we uncovered that will be drawn out later?

Maybe, if social marginalisation was recognised through the backbone of criminal justice, restorative justice would be easier to sell to the public. Various studies have shown that restorative justice is effective and less costly and the government's own analysis of this research has concluded that it reduces the frequency of reoffending by 14 per cent (Restorative Justice Council, 2013). Restorative justice is a means of bringing perpetrators and victims together to resolve harm caused by offences. This would seem far more inclusive and make a child that has fallen off track feel valued by the village that they live in, bearing in mind that the village has often failed to make that child's environment safe and nurturing. We will look at one real-life example of the effectiveness of restorative justice in *Chapter 6*.

We are all responsible for the environment in which children are growing, and for how they develop within that environment. I understand that it is a hard sell to the British public, however the youth justice system needs to be tough enough to not pander to the public and instead develop an alternative narrative. Lead by example and others will follow. This doesn't exclude victims of crime and their experience of harm, which is often the interpretation of the public when we describe children who offend as 'victims.' It just means we are living in villages that are creating too many victims, harm and pain and we need to rethink the environments these children are growing-up in to keep them and others safe. The last thing villagers should be doing is blaming children if they are, as the good doctor describes, experiencing a biological response to developmental trauma, exposure to criminality and are attachment survivors. We now know enough about the consequences of harm growing-up in some of our most disadvantaged communities can have on our most vulnerable children. More credit needs to be given to those families in these villages not having these negative outcomes for their children, as opposed to claims that other families or children lack resilience.

However we look at it, I would describe these children as victims of relational harm: harm not prevented by the adults in the village. 'Their environment is often what led them to offend' (Burke, 2016) with adult relationships being their environment. It should be about reducing the number of victims, not defaulting to a position of making the child feel solely responsible for factors outside his or her control. Even former chair of the Youth Justice Board, Charlie Taylor (2016, p. 17) found that 'Evidence suggests that contact with the justice system can have a tainted effect on children, i.e. it makes them more, rather than less likely to reoffend.' Then we use words like disengagement when we seemingly have the paradoxical effect to the one we set out to achieve. Maybe the youth justice system through the eyes of the child's experience has always been a system that is focused on punishing them. This is a perception that can be changed by employing those from their own communities with similar backgrounds and experiences, and making the youth justice system an extension of their village.

According to Ministry of Justice data (2016), 42 per cent of adult prisoners had experienced school exclusion and 25 per cent had experienced being removed from their family and placed in local authority care. When we discuss the adult prison system, there really are too many variations and correlating factors showing why adults end up in prison. However, this data does demonstrate a significant link between many, but not all, of those that enter both children's targeted services and those that enter prison as adults. We maybe need to think about the cost of trying to change these identities throughout a lifespan against the cost of investing properly in preventing people developing criminal identities in the first instance. Structural inequality perpetuates disadvantaged children's experience of both relational and economic poverty. Although children's services and the professionals within them try and work hard to mitigate the cycle of criminality, the data of those that experience youth custody and the recent acknowledgment of child exploitation indicates serious limitations on modifying lots of children's life trajectories before they enter custody, or keeping them safe from exposure to criminality.

When we consider that almost half of the young offender institution population have experienced care, it would suggest that the village has in fact let them down. It seems we are locking-up the very children that are least able to obtain relational support, either due to their criminal identities or behavioural issues developed due to factors they simply could not understand or comprehend. Let's remember that prisons make good prisoners, not good citizens. Also, if 25 per cent of adult prisoners have spent time in care (above), I wonder the percentage of those that have had social care involvement at some stage during their development. Being taken into care is often a very last resort for children, so the true number is likely to be much higher. Taylor (2017, p. 16) in his review of youth justice stated that he had 'spoken to many local authority leaders who want the freedom to integrate their youth offending services with their children, family, youth and mental health provision, and to work differently with education, health, social care and housing services.' However, it seems to me that the youth justice system needs to become an integrated part of the village to truly be effective in changing identities and gaining the trust of the children we are trying to connect with and change. It is such an institutional way of thinking to talk about the interface or partnerships of services and organizations and not mention the children's community. We will be exploring this further in *Chapter 5,* 'The Risk Switch.'

Some concluding comments

It was fascinating as a justice professional to explore my own personal journey in detail, reflecting on the factors at play which led me into the youth justice system to the point of incarceration aged just 17. I found the whole process was wrapped up around relationships. Whether it was the relationship with my mother after she had experienced abuse, neglect and removal from her family relationships or the lack of relationship with an absent father which left me seeking any male role model that showed me attention. Or the relational experiences mum exposed me to with people addicted to drugs, involved in violence or with behavioural problems which included but were not solely related to criminality. But also, the lack of attachments to supportive adults, maybe in school or in the community because we were also constantly moving. This was hardly ever spoken about during my journey through the justice system, other than a few words in a report for court. I only truly understood my childhood adversity when I learnt about and understood the language professionals use.

It seems that children develop their identity through relationships. They are exposed to harm through relationships. They experience rejection through relationships. If this is the case, surely the response from institutions should be to buffer these experiences through relationships. This is what we will explore through the coming chapters as well as how to be in a relationship with a child caught up in this relational mess. In this context, every contact is an opportunity to be that relational buffer. A child will know if you're present enough to recognise and believe their internal fight with themselves. Especially once they start to feel, as I did, that they are a child the village doesn't want. This risks pushing them off into the arms of those they *can* relate to if we do not connect with them. Crime often comes when they have decided they belong on the outside of the village and its rules. When they lose connection with those that should and could have protected them from relational harm.

To draw this chapter to a close, I want you to re-visit the statement at the start of it that, 'It takes a village to raise a child.' This is an Igbo and Yoruba proverb that exists in many different African languages. Then think about a courtroom when a child is often told they don't take responsibility for their actions. Having been one of those children, it felt like I was a rabbit caught in headlights, more fearful of the system itself than those that had coerced me into selling drugs and made it abundantly clear that I was to 'keep my mouth shut' whilst on remand for 'our' crimes.

It is worth thinking about a quote from Dr Dan Siegal which really captures most of what we have covered in this chapter. 'Of all the factors in human life that predict the best positive outcomes, supportive relationships are number 1' (Siegal, 2013). When it comes to young people in trouble, it is our responsibility as the villagers to provide that relationship. Let's continue to explore what seem to be the barriers to providing relational support to this group of young people. If we better understand the complexities that create barriers, we will be better placed to overcome them.

CHAPTER 3

Don't Judge a Book by Its Cover

Let's explore relationships between those who enter the youth and criminal justice systems due to their behaviour, and those who experience it through employment. We know inequality and social marginalisation exist within society, but how do they affect relationships within the justice system? This is a key question as no organization or service can exist outside of the societal structure it operates within. This chapter is a critical analysis of those relationships and looks at whether the support that is offered from a position of privilege is received in a reciprocal way from those placed in disadvantage.

Most justice organizations responsible for reducing crime would claim that building relationships with service recipients is fundamental to helping young people and adults desist from crime (see, e.g. Youth Justice Board, 2019). This is because it is imperative for helping the disadvantaged, who disproportionately make up those involved with justice services, to gain better life outcomes and crime-free lives. Where service providers are unable or unwilling to build empathetic and compassionate relationships with those receiving services, it is unlikely that they will be effective in achieving their aim of changing behaviours. Given the current positive justice model 'Child Fist, Offender Second' within youth justice (Case, 2015), the 'offender' label is less important for children in conflict with the law than adults, therefore increasing the importance of relationship building. If we are focusing primarily on the 'child' part of this model, we have to link this to what we know about child development. We must provide relationships first as they are the key factor to engagement. Without engagement, or indeed connection, risk management and assessment processes are unlikely to effect change.

In children's social work theory this is defined as 'relationship-based practice' (Murphy, 2013) which focuses on the importance of relationship building between service provider and recipient. However, in his conclusion, Murphy also explains that a 'person-centred relationship-based approach to contemporary social work is untenable.' He describes contemporary social work as too directive in practice, making it State-centred, not person-centred. Mainly because it can be directive of parents through assessment and plans with the threat of punitive measures such as children being removed or court proceedings if they are unable or unwilling to comply. A relationship-based approach anchored in person-centred principles is one of being non-directive. In my considerable experience on both sides of youth justice, there is often a contradiction in this field too. If we want to place relationships at the heart of the youth justice system, we need to think about how the system itself functions and whether it allows for a person-centred, relationship-based approach with children or young people requiring exactly that.

As we explored in *Chapter 2*, relationships are fundamental to the development of a child's identity. They are fundamental to our sense of self, our connection with others and, more often than not, how children experience harm during their developmental years. In the words of Dr Karen Treisman (2018), 'When developmental trauma happens in the context of relationships, the healing has to happen in the context of relationships.' It makes perfect sense to me that the answer is most likely to be found in the hearts of others and is achieved through human connection and building trusting relationships. Kindness, compassion, understanding and empathy are often lacking or significantly reduced where developmental trauma happens. Therefore, this is the feast of ingredients that these young people need to recover, or at least to start the healing process from their past harms. In *Chapter 7*, we explore whether youth crime has a relationship or connection with complex trauma or childhood adversity and if so in what context.

Being exposed to criminality which shapes a child's identity is defined as an adversity within Felitti et als' 'Adverse Childhood Experiences (ACE) Study' (1998) but, rightly so, is not viewed through the lens of developmental trauma itself. However, when you are excluded from school, gravitate towards those with criminal identities or end up in prison as a result of that exposure, believe me when I say so, these societal responses are traumatic for the young person, whether a result of their behaviour or not. Whether the shaping of the child's criminal identity is or is not a trauma, I believe the response of society to the child can contribute to developmental harm, a confused sense of self, social rejection and isolation. So maybe when we are exploring the term child criminal exploitation, exposure to criminality should be part of the discussion which we will look at in detail in *Chapter 6,* 'Joint Enterprise.'

I spent a decade as a young man receiving a justice service as a result of my behaviour through court, probation and prison. I have also spent 14 years working in youth justice, children's services and even a secure children's home during the Covid-19 crisis. These experiences have provided me with what I believe is a unique insight into the key components and barriers to relationship building with young people in trouble. If you asked my wife, Tamara, she will tell you I speak about nothing else but how the youth justice system could be more effective at building relationships with this group. I see inequality through a lens that has shaped my practice over the years, and I inevitably build relationships with young people in trouble as a result of sharing that unique perspective and vantage point of service delivery.

I came to work in the youth justice system because I wanted to use my personal experience of changing my own behaviour and improving my life outcomes to help other young people in trouble to improve theirs. I wanted to help them *before* they experienced custody, knowing how this had such a negative impact on my self-perception. My reason for writing this book is because, having now been a youth justice professional for 14 years, I feel relationships have somehow become a secondary thought after industrial process, strategy and structure. I also feel there is not enough training by those with lived experience to share their perspective of the system itself which is required to improve its relational effectiveness. Just to be clear, lived experience isn't only being involved in crime and recovering, which is why it is 'lived' as opposed to 'living.' This is in fact a less significant component from my view; it is experiencing the system itself that brings insight and a perspective from which services could benefit, i.e. by employing such individuals and allowing them a seat at the table. I don't believe it is enough to consult with individuals currently experiencing services as they are often still in the 'living' part of their journey. We will critically analyse the *why* in *Chapter 7.*

Before we go further about how relationships affect young people in trouble, I want to share a short story with you. Take a moment to picture this experience in your mind. I was once asked to visit Oxford University to spend some time with their world leading Professor in Paediatric Neuromuscular Diseases.

I was introduced to their spouse and they both walked me around to show me how wonderful it was for them to share their work and personal life at this great university. The three of us were then stopped by a homeless person in the street and asked for change which we politely declined and moved on due to feeling a little uncomfortable. I got home and reflected on my day and how wonderful all the people were that showed me around the university …. and how I could have given that homeless person some change.

Take a moment to think about the instant mental associations you made in your mind while reading that paragraph, towards the characters involved. Was the professor a black female with a nose piercing and Mohican? Was her partner a 30-year-old Muslim woman with a headscarf? Was the homeless person a well-kept female dressed from head to toe in a Gucci outfit? If this was true, I would be highly surprised and vast amounts of research demonstrates this not to be the case. It is okay to create associations as this is how the brain functions and it does so based on our experiences in life. Making these associations has kept us safe as a human race for generations through evolution. The question is, how do these association, assumptions and often prejudices play a role in relationships, specifically in the justice system?

There are various research studies that have defined this function as *implicit bias* (e.g. Greenwald, 2006). Making assumptions may have kept us safe over generations of evolution, however implicit bias also comes with negative consequences such as overt and covert racism, prejudices and discrimination. We should define the term and the science behind the theory before exploring this further. Social psychologists Mahzarin Banaji and Tony Greenwald first coined the term implicit bias in the 1990s. It grew in popularity in 1998, when Banaji and Greenwald developed the well-known Implicit Association Test (IAT) to confirm their hypothesis. Since the Black Lives Matter movement has responded to the killing of black man George Floyd by a police officer in the USA in 2020, with my colleagues I have been requested to undertake Unconscious Bias training which is a recognition that services understand its importance on practice and service delivery. The Executive Director of Safe Places for the Advancement of Community and Equity (SPACE), Dushaw Hockett, explains bias to be a preference for, or prejudice against, a group of people. In his TEDx talk (2017), he explains the science that makes a bias 'implicit,' of which there are fundamentally three characteristics. These are:

- it operates at the subconscious level;
- it often runs contrary to our conscious beliefs; and
- has rapid automatic mental associations that we often don't control.

Implicit bias

Implicit bias has been argued as disproportionately affecting people of colour, people that are not native to the majority of a country, or other minority groups. Lammy (2016) in his work exploring disproportionality found that 51 per cent of Black and Minority Ethnic (BAME) people felt the criminal justice system discriminates against particular groups and individuals, as against 35 per cent of the British-born white population. This is reflected in the fact that he also found that 'despite making up just 14 per cent of the population, BAME men and women make up 25 per cent of the prison population.' Overt racism is hard to find in modern-day Britain, although it still of course exists. However, many believe that such figures highlight that in fact structural inequality and implicit bias contribute to these numbers. Black Lives Matter is a movement created to address the issue of how the black community in particular has experienced bias historically. This is of course connected with the history of slavery, but this community continue to experience social exclusion and discrimination today. However, nowadays it seems to be more implicit, institutional and systemic which in my view is harder to highlight and challenge due to its more subtle nature. I believe similar issues apply across class and certainly this impacts on disconnects between support services and communities.

I have experienced what I believe to be implicit bias on both sides of the criminal justice fence due to group membership. I have witnessed first-hand what I believe are relational barriers between the groups on either side of the justice system. In 1971, Dr Philip Zimbardo conducted the Stanford Prison Experiment. They selected middle-class students and assigned them roles in a mock prison as officers and prisoners to explore the potential conflict between these two groups. The experiment was not completed due to psychological torture inflicted by some officers towards the inmates. The experiment was designed to highlight the nature of the relationship between these two groups, being complex and adversarial and that it impacted on power dynamics.

This social psychology experiment attempted to investigate the psychological effects of perceived power, focusing on the struggle between prisoners and prison officers. One of the conclusions was that 'social and ideological factors determined how both groups behaved, with individuals acting in a way that they thought was required, rather than using their own judgement.' The research was a field experiment, not a scientific one and has had many critics, but nonetheless it does provide an example of how quickly factions develop on both sides of the justice system when individuals are assigned set roles within it. This inevitably influences implicit bias. Given I have worked in a secure setting and been an inmate in one, I have experienced this reality on both sides and believe it is a significant factor leading to the high prison population and also high reoffending rates in England and Wales (Prison Reform Trust, 2019).

Youth Justice Board guidance (2019) states 'high quality relationships established with children and their parents/carers are vital for effective assessment and planning.' Relationships are therefore the vehicle to achieving the desired outcome of a very expensive system. In my opinion, relationships within justice organizations would benefit from being afforded more consideration, training and continued personal development. The same level of consideration as risk-assessment, risk-management and report writing. If justice services get relationships right it is in the best interests of the whole country. There are multiple reasons for this:

- It will keep children safe from exposure to crime and becoming criminalised as young as ten-years-old.
- We will reduce crime, and as a result, victims of crime.
- We will make the country a safer, healthier place to live.
- We will save unnecessary spending by the taxpayer on dealing with crime—and so lower the cost of police officers, the courts system, prisons, youth justice and probation.
- We will develop trust between communities many that offend come from and authority.

When professionals and services take relational experiences for granted in the justice system by stating they are genuine, honest and non-judgemental, this doesn't go far enough. We need to fully-understand how we are all also shaped by our life experiences and how this affects our interaction, or how we share relational spaces with service recipients in a justice context driven primarily by risk-management processes.

Can implicit bias impact on relationships with those who come into contact with the justice system? I first started to consider this when I began working as a professional within youth justice. I was continuously hearing language which was divisive on both sides and felt a natural personal internal conflict. I identified as an ex-offender more when non ex-offenders used the term (a label I tend not to use so far as possible, but it is relevant in this explanation) now I was a paid justice professional which was an interesting experience. Just like in the Stanford Prison Experiment, I witnessed how people were assigned roles on both sides and, as a result, used words like 'these kids' or even 'our kids' placing labels on the young people, often unintentionally but in my view with unintended consequences. The young people would say, 'You lot' or 'Them' and early in my career I was told by a young man, 'Andi, you're one of us, not one of them.' This drove me even harder to prove this not to be the case but affected my confidence in being a professional nonetheless. When in prison we used the term 'pen pushers' a lot and yet here I am writing a book about crime which in the eyes of many current prisoners may mean I am in fact a 'pen pusher.' The term is often applied to justice professionals because we write things about 'them' down which is often used against them later.

Reflecting on this takes me back to a cognitive behavioural therapy (CBT) course I participated in whilst serving a two-year term in HM Prison Lindholme. The facilitators were two middle-class white female assistant psychologists that were slightly older than me, aged just 22. I was constantly in conflict with their programme content because I felt that they had not walked a mile in my shoes. It was my own implicit bias because I knew nothing about them, other than my own perceptions which were born out of my own personal experience that made me feel they couldn't understand me and my life experiences. Granted that in part this was to justify my behaviour to myself at the time! It wasn't so much me not taking responsibility as much as I didn't at that point have the capacity to understand the *why* to my behaviour, so I leapt to put things in context unwittingly without the ability to articulate this, as I can now. I was trying in an uneducated way to express or link my relational experiences as a developing child to my substance abuse and how this shaped my gravitation to specific relationships that I felt would accept me. However, being a dysregulated and traumatised young man, I couldn't manage the conversation and the facilitators clearly weren't attuned to me in a way that was required. This then led to my frustration, fuelling my view of them as pen-pushers. So they wrote down that I was challenging and referred me onto another course. This shuts prisoners down and they learn that they are not heard and understood. Prisoners are the experts in their life journeys, our job as professionals is to help them develop their own narrative in a constructive way, not close them down if they disagree with our model or perspective.

I now know most of what they were delivering was grounded in an evidence base because I am trained to deliver CBT programmes to young offenders. A lot of the course was focused on the principle of group membership, examining my implicit bias and peer group association which contributed to my offending behaviour. They were absolutely right about my gravitation to negative relationships, but what was missing in their programme was the 'why.' If they'd focused on that, their efforts wouldn't have been experienced as a blame and shame intervention. Also, they were delivering the information or challenging my views before building a foundation of relational trust. You see, you can't access the pre-frontal cortex (the thinking part of the brain), which is what they were attempting to do, without first connecting with the limbic system (the emotional part of the brain). No matter how skilled you are, if someone doesn't feel safe or they feel judged by you or the programme you are delivering, their mind will become closed to the information you're providing. Human connection first, programme information second. Dr Bruce Perry (2020) explains this as 'regulate, relate, reason' in his 'Network Stress and Trauma' video. The cortex can switch off in a stressed or anxious state without a feeling of connection and safety with the individual they are connecting or communicating with.

I needed them to explain to me why I felt a safe human connection to people in prison and little more than shame and judgement when in the company of folk like them. They consistently refused to have this discussion with me in any detail which left me feeling that they didn't understand and then my mind closed off to their programme content. We have explored how criminal identity is in part shaped by relationships, so it wasn't the content of the programme that needed to change but the context of the relationship they built with me and how the content of the programme was delivered. If they had been more curious about my personal experiences, and I had felt they better understood, maybe they would have seen the world through my lens and not been over reliant on their evidence base. Instead, I felt that they assumed they knew my story but focused on my behaviour, and that made me feel judged.

A Dan Siegal (2014) saying springs to mind which is, 'Treat people as if they are where they ought to be and you will help them become what they are capable of being.' Treat people as if you can change their behaviour as a result of justice research (which by the way changes as often as I change my socks) and you are likely to close them down.

Just like in the Stanford Prison Experiment, I was assigning myself a role and they didn't seem to have the relational skills to bring down the divisive wall between us. The truth is, it was incredibly unlikely that they had experienced the level of adversity, lack of relational resource or support and intergenerational trauma I had. However, this is beside the point. The point was that I was unconsciously exposing my implicit bias towards the group that they represented, which was grounded in my own lived experience. I felt school had rejected me and, since that point, and as no-one that behaved or spoke like they did accepted me or built a relationship with me personally, or only when they were paid to, it felt like a judgement intervention and incarceration. But exploiters and violent people did without judgement, so where does a young person with behavioural problems turn?

From being a very young child I always felt more deprived than others I knew, even when living in deprived areas intoxicated with poverty. I was then removed from my mother and placed in care which was followed shortly after that by school exclusion, drug addiction, criminal exploitation and prison, all before I reached the grand old age of 18. These experiences left me feeling rejected by not only the academic and what I perceived to be middle-class world, but also anyone that I associated with authority. This led to me experiencing the justice system at that time through the lens of a victim as much as a perpetrator. I am not arguing that I was right, just the only way to break down this wall of fear is though human connection and relationships, not assessments or programmes.

Although professionals recognised the impact of my childhood experiences, it often came across that most believed they wouldn't have had the same outcome, given that set of circumstances. I believe I needed to hear a restorative response, even when I had committed an offence—for them to have said, 'That is not okay and should not have happened to you.' However, the language in a justice context is often, 'This young person doesn't take responsibility.' It took me into my thirties to understand the relational context to my behaviour which makes sense when we think about brain maturity.

Newsweek (Requarth, 2016) discussed the issue of juvenile incarceration in the US and brain development. B J Casey, Director of the Sackler Institute for Developmental Psychobiology at Cornell's Weill Medical College states that 'Brain areas involved in reasoning and self-control, such as the prefrontal cortex, are not fully developed until the mid-20s—a far later age than previously thought.' In the same article, Laurence Steinberg, a Professor of Psychology states that, in a justice context, 'It's not about guilt or innocence... The question is, "how culpable are they, and how do we punish them?".'

If you speak to many justice professionals they will state that people involved in offending often view themselves as victims when being challenged by professionals about their behaviour. The question to ask is, why is this the case and how do we as a justice system manage this? At times we punish, incarcerate, isolate and shame those that don't engage in relationships with the establishment rather than looking at what needs to shift in how we work to engage these young people. Group membership and implicit bias is prevalent in all aspects of society, the question is do we accept this in a justice context? How can we be more proactive in changing the narrative of *they*, and *them* to *us*? I believe one way of doing that is the justice system being more inclusive of those with lived experience to help shape services in a way that reduces the othering on both sides. To develop a perception that it is not adversarial and that, even though it has to hold people to account, it still wants to have the best for those caught in it, in a visible way.

Identity, condemnation and redemption

I was never challenged about my behaviour by anyone that I felt represented my life experiences or identity. I was never told by any professional that fell into my 'in-group' that my behaviour was unacceptable or that my behaviour would likely change as I got older so I should speed the process up. This compounded my negative experience of the unfair world I perceived I lived in.

Through my lens, I was simply being told that I was entirely responsible for my behaviour and inevitably gravitated to others who were in negative cycles of behaving, but who offered me valuable relational experiences and perceived safety. This became my truth. Partly because of my inability to see things in a different way due to my childhood shaping my perspective in such a damaging way. Also, because it helped my underdeveloped brain deal with the world I was navigating and kept me safe from the shame of being alone and scared.

In desistance theory there are two scripts as formulated by Maruna (2001). The 'condemnation' script effectively increases the likelihood of reoffending because the individual feels condemned to a life of crime. They often blame their circumstances on external factors they feel they have little control over. Such things as addiction, poverty, peers or childhood experiences that were too damaging. The 'redemption' script, being the opposite, reduces the risk of reoffending as individuals within this script take responsibility for their behaviour and often have optimism about their non-offending futures. For me, the question lies in how do we effectively shift someone from one narrative to the other? As the Youth Justice Board (2019) states that relationship building is fundamental to the process, why do we have so little research into how to develop relationships with this particular group? We call out their implicit bias but never discuss that we all have our own, and offenders rarely fall into our in-group either. If we do not identify and discuss this, we are ignoring social marginalisation and relational poverty.

Young people heavily involved in offending often perceive that only those with shared experience understand their world, which helps explain the gravitation to such relationships, even though they are often unsafe. Therefore, if they are only challenged by professionals they perceive to not understand, it is likely that they will continue with othering narratives which allow them to not receive information and support. It can even have a counterproductive impact on their experience of social inclusion. They have been unable to access such relationships in their personal lives until they commit a crime and people are paid to spend time with them highlighting what we have defined as relational poverty. We are not equal in the relationships we are able to access because they are reciprocal, especially as children. If you are from a dysfunctional family, this is likely to impact on your ability to socially function or regulate and, as a result, impact your ability to access functional or regulated relationships. Trust me, I have been there and people avoid you like the plague, even in school, eventually through exclusion, which for many is compounded by family separation and care.

If your household has criminality prevalent, parents of other families with no prevalence will actively seek to prevent you from spending time with their children. This is bias, not so much implicit as just overt human protectionism of those they care most about. However, there is a victim to that relational poverty and it is often the child who can't access positive and supportive relationships. They may not be able to articulate how this feels or what it means for them but, like my experiences in primary school, they are aware they are being discriminated against and avoided. If as a result of their identity, their exposure to adversity and lack of accessible relationships they gravitate to those relationships which increase the likelihood of offending, we must understand this process is more than active life choices. By simply asking young people to change relationships that we perceive to be negative, we are ignoring the implications of social marginalisation and blaming the victims of the experience. We must recognise this when we work with this group, and understand their need for positive relational experiences that they perceive to be non-judgemental.

If parents are contributing to the child's experience of adversity due to their own un-met needs, dysfunction or dysregulation, the child is simultaneously prevented from access to relational buffers within their family as a result. Due to attachment being a survival need, the child is incredibly unlikely to betray his or her care providers and trust those in authority, because they are scared of being detached from their primary attachments. I remember this process well. I felt far more comfortable around drug addicts, criminals and violent adults because I felt they kept me safe in my perceived unsafe world. It was a normal biological response to a very unpredictable, chaotic and adverse childhood. As humans, we are biologically programmed to seek safety. I didn't know at the time but it was the very resilience I had developed to survive in my situation that would result in my incarceration and judgement of society.

I have offered insights into my own implicit bias and how it also manifests, in various ways, with many who come into contact with the justice system, often *othering* professionals that work within it. Their tendency to think this way can prevent them accessing professional support to mitigate their experiences of poverty and criminal behaviour; we really need to work on how to overcome this.

Labels, relationships, inequality

But what about professionals working with people that commit crime? We work with those who offend to ensure communities are safe, improve outcomes for them and are often skilled at establishing relationships with disadvantaged groups. We should all subscribe to the Youth Justice Board principle that relationships matter when it comes to diverting children away from crime. We expect that justice professionals will have non-judgemental approaches to young people and inclusive practice at all times. If they don't, we should expect that service managers will guide them back onto the right path. Justice professionals are human beings and as such carry implicit bias towards the people that they come into contact with in the justice system, as does everyone else.

Examples of this are the labels applied to the young people within that system often described as 'offenders,' 'risky,' 'dangerous,' 'these' youngsters or even 'our' young people. Furthermore, when the words 'our young people' are used, many don't mean the young people we have round to the home for Sunday lunch, otherwise social marginalisation wouldn't exist. It is a label applied to group the young people together as service recipients that specific professionals work with and, as it is in a justice context, it is a justice label. These alone are not discriminatory, just examples of how we can easily put people into groups on both sides of the justice fence. However, I believe it is nonetheless contributing to *othering* children that offend, as a stereotype, and placing them in another or opposing group.

Only this month someone in a senior position within youth justice told me before speaking to young people involved in youth justice that he was 'a little rusty when it comes to talking to service users.' It wasn't meant with any malice and I personally believe this was an incredibly insightful individual that fully understood inequality and relationships between service recipients and providers because we had this very discussion. The reason this statement stood out to me was because I do not differentiate between talking to a senior manager, a practitioner or a young person in trouble in this way. I never needed preparation to talk to prisoners when I was in prison, so why would I need preparation as a professional? Again, another example of implicit bias that most wouldn't even think about unless attuned to such language. It doesn't mean it is negative *per se*, just something we will not improve in the absence of service recipients breaking down these barriers or challenging this narrative.

Risk Relational Paradox

I recently heard Dr Alisha Moreland-Capuia state that 'change happens from within' at a Trauma Responsive Scotland conference. This is part of what I took away from her talk and book *Training for Change*. The main feature of this is what I call 'Risk Relational Paradox' as depicted in the diagram below (the reference to 'PACT practice' in the first inner box is to the need for presence, attunement, connection and trust as described in *Chapter 8*).

RISK RELATIONSHIP PARADOX
RELATIONAL JUSTICE PRACTICE TYPES

**Trauma-informed Relational
Justice Practitioner**

Trauma-informed Practice
ACE Aware
PACT Practice

Risk Relational Aware

Support recipients to navigate systems
Educate others about
institutional power disparity
Challenge othering of service recipients
Co-produce interventions and programmes
Value and promote Lived Experience

Risk Relational Recognition

Recognising Relational Poverty
Restorative Practice
Recognising risk of relational harm
Reflecting on own othering behaviour
Recognising institutional power disparity

Risk Relational Prevelance

Little understanding of Relational Poverty
'They don't engage'
Pathologising service recipients
Stereotyping and othering behaviour
Non-reflective practice
Risk relational ignorance

During my journey on both sides of the justice experience I have come across individuals or professionals with varying capacities, motivations and abilities to connect with young people in trouble on different levels. Some professionals are simply better at communicating, engaging and connecting with young people in trouble. Observing these individuals in different ways, I have come to the conclusion that there are quite specific differences between justice professionals that often use phrases like 'he/she doesn't engage' or 'these kids don't listen' and those that constantly reflect on their practice and recognise institutional harm. I recently heard Lisa Cherry describe this experience on Twitter as 'system trauma.' Becoming involved in a person's life who is already facing hardship and not improving their circumstances and fully-understanding how or why.

I have met wonderfully trauma-informed, relational justice practitioners on both ends of the justice experience. The Risk Relational Paradox diagram above illustrates phases that, if professionals understand and acknowledge them, will enhance their practice so they are better positioned to be relational as a result. People can of course transition forwards and also backwards due to empathy or compassion fatigue. Also, depending on where they 'are at' personally or emotionally, managers should be able to identify these phases and have a model to work from and this is one which can be reflected upon for line management and supervision (as well as personal reflection).

The diagram explains how a professional can develop through varying levels of understanding Risk Relational Paradox to becoming and maintaining trauma-informed, relational justice practice. If a practitioner is repeatedly labelling service recipients as 'non-engagers' or 'hard to reach,' they are likely lacking understanding of the complexities of Risk Relational Paradox and institutional power disparity. Managers in youth and criminal justice need to be able to identify non-reflective practitioners that need development in relationship building and to be able to provide them with the supervision required to develop their ability to connect.

If young people are frequently asking for different workers or certain practitioners use breach or sanction measures more than others, this requires the same level of training that would be provided for someone who needs to improve their report writing or develop their assessment skills. In the absence of this managerial support, the fault will always lie with the young person or service recipient. This again highlights disparity of power when we have a responsibility to provide the right relational service for the disadvantaged to accord with the requirements of the Youth Justice Board. This model can be used for peer supervision to develop discussion and collective understanding. Justice services can pair those practitioners that use all the skills in the Risk Relational Aware phase to develop the relationship building of others that require it, or who are new to a service.

Once justice practitioners recognise how Risk Relational Paradox plays a role which is often negative in terms of relationship building, they are more likely to:

- use restorative practice (see later);
- be relational;
- question how institutions impact on relationships with disadvantaged recipients;
- reflect on their own practice regularly, whether on their own or with colleagues; and
- be open about how certain offences affect their relationships with service recipients more than others.

I can offer an example of this. As a developing child, sexual perpetrators played a role in my removal from my family. My youth incarceration experience conditioned me to hold strong negative views about sex offenders or at least to disassociate from them. This required me to recognise Risk Relational Paradox to build effective relationships with young people that commit these types of offences. I reflected on my lived experience of this happening to me as a point of reference. I have since I believe had real success with this particular group of young people but, to build on my implicit bias, I first had to recognise how it plays out in relationships and this improved my relational practice as a result. It should be okay to reflect and say, 'I am not able to connect with this young person and maybe the reason lies more with me than the child or young person.' The best practitioners are the reflective practitioners.

When practitioners are Risk Relational Aware, they will confront the othering behaviours of other practitioners. This can at times be a challenge and the more risk relationally aware ones we have in a service the easier this becomes. Just like challenging racism becomes easier if more allies are available to challenge from within, Risk Relational Aware practitioners will:

- always seek to co-produce assessments and plans with recipients;
- promote the lived experience to improve service delivery through inclusion, incorporating that lens or vantage point;
- actively seek to reduce institutional power disparity;
- highlight the perspectives of those labelled hard to reach;
- most importantly understand and inform others of the impact of ACEs on the life course and social and health outcomes; and as a result

- achieve trauma-informed practice in a justice context.

This will benefit both recipient and provider and will help develop the connections and trust required to build non-judgemental connection.

The Lammy Review (2016) found black, Asian, minority and ethnic groups received more punitive justice outcomes than their white peers. Lord Lammy wouldn't have been able to explore the Risk Relational Paradox because he wasn't looking into, e.g. why the justice system had high reoffending rates or the reason there is a consistent call for prison reform, just how it affected one group more than others. However, he did expose that implicit bias does exist institutionally within the justice system towards people of colour. I have witnessed BAME people receive different sentences for similar offences to other groups both as a prisoner and as a professional, so I am sure Lord Lammy was right to reignite this discussion. The Black Lives Matter movement is on the back of every Premier League football shirt and on everyone's mind after George Floyd's death at the hands of a police officer in the USA.

The general public and the press are often vocal about their bias towards those that offend. There is, e.g. often nothing implicit about how the public views those in prison. Old adages that most of us recognise such as 'lock 'em up and throw away the key' or 'leopards never change their spots' are just two examples of how people view those with convictions. A BBC Scotland report (2018) found that 75 per cent of UK businesses wouldn't employ someone that has been to prison. Society thinks more about retribution than it does about the consequences of being defined as a risk and whether these sanctions increase or decrease the likelihood of further offending or result in more or less victims. I am not arguing that people shouldn't be managed through a risk lens, we just need to recognise the consequences, practically, relationally and socially once it has happened and how we improve equality, not compound relational poverty, once the sentence is over.

Being assessed as a risk to other people places people in a group with shared experience and the impact is difficult to understand if you haven't experienced it. Whether the behaviour requires this assessment to keep people safe is a separate point. Almost all professionals working within the justice system assess people and their risk of harm to others. This inevitably affects the service recipients' perceptions of themselves, of how they are viewed and their position within society. Justice professionals are largely unlikely to have experienced being assessed as a risk to others. There is of course no shame in that. I still live with the consequences today so I am envious. In fact, I was risk-assessed only last week even though I have now been crime-free for almost two decades. It does however inevitably create a sense of division and othering, particularly by those that have not had much experience of offending in their personal lives, so we need to think about how to talk about that and not ignore it. If our brain works in a way that makes instant judgements, often contrary to our beliefs, how can behaviour that you disagree with and causes harm not effect the relational space?

Now, we have those that assess risk and those assessed as a risk and as long as they build positive relationships they can all work together for better outcomes, right? This is a critical point in the relationship building process within a justice context. Are people in the justice system always open and honest about the relationships they have with clients? In probation, it is clearer: relationships are important; everyone knows where they stand. However, when it comes to young people in youth justice:

- Is the conversation as open due to the age of the young people?;
- Are the boundaries always as clear?;
- How does it feel for a young person or child to only come into contact with safe adults in a professional's context when they wouldn't come into contact with this within their personal relationships?;
- How does it feel when the contact is primarily due to the fact that a professional is assessing the risk you pose to others?;
- What does the relationship with the 'system' and the varying levels of understanding of practitioners within it feel like for a young person or child?; and
- If everyone has a different understanding of Risk Relational Paradox does that affect the relationship young people have with other professionals that understand it well?

Summary

We will later in this book interview those with lived experience now mature enough to understand their childhoods, the system and the consequences of being in it. They have had enough time away from the justice system to reflect and ponder about what worked, what didn't work and whether the justice experience was positive, negative or both. We have already:

- taken a journey through the challenges of how children often develop criminal identities through relationships;
- explored how relationships or a lack of them can leave a child at risk of developing a criminal identity and why they gravitate to others that pose a risk to their wellbeing;
- explored the communities young people in trouble are often growing-up in and how those communities (their 'village') can contribute and protect children from developing criminal identities;
- explored how relationships, or a lack of them, leave children at risk or otherwise of being shaped to avoid support services;
- demonstrated the relational challenges when risk of harm is present and how implicit bias often creates a barrier to building relationships through my model of Risk Relational Paradox; and
- seen how this includes barriers to relationship building with young people in trouble and how young people often feel when coming into contact with the justice system itself.

Does the youth justice system and the mechanisms within it mitigate everything discussed above to enable practitioners to navigate these things and concentrate on relationships? How does risk-management and the processes that come with that lend its hand to providing a relational context for youth justice practitioners to reduce such complex barriers? It seems to me that in many cases there is a lot of mistrust and barriers to be broken down, which obviously takes time if human connections are built on trust. If relationships are a significant factor as to why young people enter the system, and relationships are fundamental to achieving desistance, surely the youth justice system, from top to bottom, should provide a platform for relationships to flourish.

The next chapter explores these very questions. So let's take a unique perspective through the lens of the recipients, the literature and my own duel perspective as we dive into some of the depths to find answers.

CHAPTER 4

A Unique Perspective of Relational Justice

Since joining the youth justice service as a professional, I have assimilated and observed various practices from my colleagues and friends. With my personal experience and connections with young people (younger peers in my case), I believe I have been in a strong position to tune into what works with the young people. Observation of the best practices then enhanced my natural ability to be present for young people in trouble in a professional context and build trusting relationships. This chapter is an observation by someone with an insight of having lived and worked on both sides of the youth justice fence.

What is the most effective way for justice practitioners to connect with young people in trouble? I have outlined why the relational process should never be taken for granted. Research has found that 'most justice systems deal predominantly with offenders from working-class backgrounds (including indigenous and ethnic minority people), and thereby reflect the class biases in definitions of social harm and crime, as well as basing responses on these biases' (White, 2015). Reflecting on my lived experience within this 'class bias control' (so-called), these are some of my thoughts and experiences on what makes for best practice in a very complex relational sphere.

There are various mechanisms within the youth justice system and each plays its individual part in achieving its individual outcomes. But youth justice doesn't operate in a vacuum. The system operates alongside other agencies and partners to achieve better outcomes for young people in trouble. The youth justice system is itself a multi-agency operation which includes health, police, education, social care and probation. After transitioning from one side to the other, my observation is that relationship building with disadvantaged groups, particularly young people, needs further exploration in detail within the context of an institutional response. By institutional, I mean risk-management processes, policies, planning and intervention models, practice models and service strategies. Relationship building within a risk context and developing trust is extremely difficult and should never been taken lightly as we have already determined.

We have also already explored the view of the previous chair of the Youth Justice Board, Charlie Taylor (2016) in his review of the youth justice system: that contact with youth justice services increases the likelihood of offending, it doesn't decrease it. Having experienced youth justice and even the adult prison estate as a service recipient, I remain convinced that, if the human connection is built on a foundation of trust, professionals can improve outcomes for young people in trouble, regardless of the reason they come into contact with them. I have no doubt that perceived risk is paradoxical to developing trusting relationships and I have already outlined and critically analysed the intricate factors for this. However, I have witnessed various justice practitioners achieve trusting relationships with this group for over a decade. I have capitalised on the components they employ to obtain that trust to improve my own knowledge, practice and skills. My lived experience provided me with a foundation, or similar vantage point of the world and justice system as the young people I now work with. However, observation of the most effective, relational colleagues in the 'restorative city' of Leeds where I work has also enhanced my ability to connect in a professional setting.

How do practitioners build relationships?

I am interested in how justice practitioners build relationships with young people within a context of what some perceive as institutional and structural inequality. A justice practitioner spending time with a young person through a statutory court order doesn't equate to a relationship, and if any practitioner believes that it does their view comes from a position of privilege. The best practitioners I have observed on both sides of the justice fence recognise, understand and respond to this complexity on an emotional level, not just a practice, theoretical or academic one. Understanding young people that enter the youth justice system experience 'intersectionality' and often view justice practitioners as authority figures to fear due to sanction and risk. Intersectionality being the interconnected nature and accumulated social prejudices and vulnerabilities, which impact on self-worth, sense of belonging and identity.

Contact with the justice system and the professionals assessing their 'risk of harm' to others compounds these experiences of powerlessness, social exclusion and being labelled as someone society deems to be an outsider. I believe this to be a contributing factor to what Taylor (2016) was pointing out in his review. Risk Relational Paradox (*Chapter 3*) isn't something that is often discussed when we explore labels such as 'offender' or 'criminal.' This is often a blind spot within the system. Once someone obtains employment within any service, their belief will more often than not be that they are automatically improving the lives of those they serve, which is on the face of it a completely reasonable position to take up. We have already explored that implicit bias often happens contrary to our beliefs and also subconsciously. These biases will be different for different practitioners but service recipients come into contact with these varying levels of bias throughout their journey, and we are finely attuned to who has them. We will see examples of this in *Chapter 6*. However, if justice practitioners are present and available on a human level, rather than an institutional one, and understand the complex difference in the child's vantage point of the system and their own, I have witnessed first-hand that this complexity can be mitigated or buffered. So, what must we recognise I hear you say?

The American psychiatrist and expert in childhood trauma Dr Bruce Perry in his talk 'Born for Love' (2016) explains that the neurological pathways in a child's brain are developed or changed through repetition. The brain develops in a use-dependant way, so experience plays a huge role in how children develop neural pathways and their subsequent ways of relating. Repetitive experiences of empathy, compassion, social perspective or consequential thinking and even language build pathways though experience of relationships. Childhood adversity and trauma as we will explore in *Chapter 7* impact on relational capacity. They shape our internal working model and view of the world—with some young people, e.g. people are not to be trusted, indeed are out to hurt and the world is an unsafe place. Therefore, we can only develop or change these neural pathways through the relational experience and repetition. If the predisposition of a young person is that others are not to be trusted, gaining their trust while at the same time assessing the risk they pose and using external controls makes connections all the more difficult.

When examining the centrality of engagement in positive youth justice, Case and Haines (2014, p. 159) found an

'inherent irony of Youth Justice Practice in England and Wales, shaped and driven by risk-based assessment and intervention, is the nature [of] its "engagement" processes (for example, court ordered contact, programmes and interventions) serve to disengage the target population (that is, children) from participation, commitment and compliance with youth justice practitioners and practice.'

Their description is that the

'current structures, mechanisms, systems and foci of youth justice in England and Wales at best inhibit, and at worst deny, the opportunity of engagement by those children targeted by them, making a radical rethinking about children's engagement with the YJS both manifest and pressing.'

They believe that the risk-assessment process can disengage justice professionals too. I can say that I was, and that I am still, incredibly grateful for the opportunity granted to me by the youth justice system when I became a professional with my background, because it demonstrates a belief that I could make a difference to children's lives. However, changing children's behaviours seems to be part of that difference making because Case and Haines are absolutely right. The best practitioners in youth justice are the ones that can see our training and processes are at times a barrier to engagement and are able to navigate this complexity. It also has to be said that the assessment tool has improved since their research took place. It is more inclusive of children's views and places more focus on strengths. However, although this is progress, I still believe we have some way to go until the system is relational. A long way to go before the system becomes engaging for both children and professionals, which will create a space for development through repetition and authentic relationships. Not a risk and process-focused system of office professionals and complicated assessments that cannot be co-produced because they are too complex for children and families to understand.

Facilitating change

Change happens through social interaction and connection within communities and relationships. As the youth justice system's structures and functions are primarily led by *risk-management,* which leads to external controls via assessments, plans and supervision, relationships and human connection need to become the vehicle to navigate these processes. Collaborative and inclusive approaches cannot be emphasised enough. Nor emotional attunement as described by Connolly (2015), using all of our senses to understand what others are feeling, so much so that we feel it too. It takes being able to sense, interpret and respond to someone so that he or she doesn't feel alone any longer or unsafe in our company.

My entry into the juvenile prison system as a 17-year-old was a lonely and incredibly scary experience which left me feeling unsafe. Every time I came across a prison officer or justice professional, I felt a sense of safety from a position of isolation. Of course, I am not advocating custody for young people, far from it. I am simply highlighting that the officers were presented with a real opportunity to build trust and connection if they were attuned, every time our paths crossed. Therefore, it can happen under any circumstances. However, I can honestly say that it didn't happen often enough to make the incarceration experience relational, due to what I believe was the lack of attunement and connection of many prison officers. Again this was, I believe, as a result of Risk Relational Paradox. Professionals available for emotional attunement when young people travel through the justice system tend to alleviate negative emotions such as shame and guilt through their relationship.

On a societal level, many of the young people that enter the justice system, certainly those that make up the population of prolific and serious young offenders or those incarcerated, have experienced intersectionality of childhood adversity, racism, inequality and educational or social rejection in their early lives. We find that they have fought through numerous life adversities which for many has created feelings of disillusionment and exclusion from the very society that has been shaped for them by adults. They then enter the youth justice system that defines them by the *risk they pose* when the *risk to them* has often been missed or not identified or modified by services. It is therefore incredibly difficult to control them or change their identity at a time when they are least likely to be influenced by professionals and more likely to be so by their peer relationships and social environments.

Risk in terms of young people is defined into three categories in youth justice: risk of reoffending (level of desistance); risk of serious harm to others; and risk of safety and wellbeing which is effectively harm to themselves or by others through behaviour. A youth justice system that is primarily led by risk-management and external control of young people creates a barrier to relationship building as found by Case and Haines (2014). When someone is presented to you as a *risk to others* this is not the foundation for any individuals to use as the basis for relationship building or trust (which we have established as 'Risk Relational Paradox').

When young people enter the justice system, they have to navigate their relationship with professionals assessing their risk and sharing this information with agencies such as the police and children's social care which they often fear. They fully-understand that lots of what happens in their daily lives and the lives of many around them they care for will be interpreted as negative or risky and, as a result, they themselves or those they care for will be demonised or sanctioned. This is often due to what (White, 2015) was describing as a *class bias response*. Often developed within cultural differences between many that shape services in this complex space and many that come into contact with it as recipients. This is a factor in why co-production of assessments, processes and even inspections must vitally be inclusive of the vantage points of service recipients. Meanwhile, the relationships that contribute to the young people's offending, with those who are often anti-establishment, encourage the young people to view justice professionals as the people that are out to harm them. Nonetheless, as described in the Risk Relational Paradox diagram, lots of justice practitioners are able to be trauma-informed relational justice practitioners and help the young people navigate this complexity. In my experience on both sides of the justice fence, many of them obtain this trust by understanding this complexity and following the key components of PACT (Presence, Attunement, Connection and Trust) discussed in *Chapter 8.*

Families that are not impacted by toxic stress, relation poverty, relational criminality or social exclusion are socially conditioned to avoid crime, violence and risk, of course. Just ask what your parents would have said if you'd brought Jack, released from a sentence for armed robbery or shoplifting, home for

Sunday dinner. Young people who enter the youth justice system, particularly those who offend persistently or seriously and enter custody, have long before experienced relational poverty and social rejection based on their constructed identity. This is often what creates their perception of professionals not caring or not wanting the best for young people in trouble. It is not always the engagement skills or even character of the professional. I often made my mind up about a probation officer before I even entered the building. They were only paid to work with me and wouldn't have done so otherwise and they 'will tell the police' what I am doing. This barrier can be difficult to break down. Nevertheless, the best way to do this is to prove to the young person that you are available to connect, not just to assess their risk, which is often their preconceived position.

The Centre for Justice Innovation (2017) found that,

'prosecuting young people or using out-of-court disposals for low-level and first-time offending does not control crime. Research has consistently shown that deepening involvement in the justice system actually makes this group more likely to reoffend.'

This is a similar statement to that made by Taylor (2016) which we have already looked at. It is often claimed that this is due to labelling and the impact of convictions which prevent access to opportunities for young people. I have to continuously disclose my previous offences and be risk-assessed if ever I apply for work with young people, or within the justice system. Therefore, I understand this argument as much as anyone else. However, it is not just the labels or social constructs which impact on our self-worth. If justice practitioners are not relational, trauma-informed or restorative in their approach, it can create a relational space which leaves the child feeling stigmatised and pathologised for normal working-class behaviour through a risk lens. This is not a 'child first' approach. When this is noticed by managers or colleagues, these individuals should be trained to improve their relational practice. This applies to those that work for the police, youth justice, the courts or any other justice agency because the impact is paradoxical to better outcomes for young people and safer communities.

Getting the balance right

Not getting the balance right between risk-management and relationships can be detrimental on a multitude of levels. Not fully-understanding or recognising the relational barriers of contact with the justice system and the insidious effects of the 'Risk Relational Paradox' can lead to an othering experience by young people. They may feel defined through a risk lens and this experience impacts on their self-worth and social inclusion. Almost every young person I have worked with within the youth justice system has continually stated that they are at 'probation' when on the phone to their friends. It is often claimed this is due to the young person feeling probation is cooler than youth justice in the eyes of their peers. However, while we primarily work with young people through a risk lens, it seems there is very little difference seen in their community, which is what's important if we want to understand more about their world view and how to reach them effectively in our practice. If we don't succeed, others with similar world views to theirs will capitalise on their vulnerability as we will explore in *Chapter 5*, 'The Risk Switch.'

As we have established, harnessing relationships at the heart of what we do should always be the primary aim of anyone working with young people in trouble to assist them to improve their behaviour. Not retribution, not getting them to take responsibility, referrals or even reparation. These secondary concepts are only likely to effect change in young people if they are delivered within the primary relational context, otherwise the young people may attend through enforcement, but neural repetition is unlikely. Reprogramming neural networks that have been developed through relationships and experiences won't be achieved through education programmes or risk-management processes, no matter how *evidence-based* we believe they are. This is just not how neural networks develop. This would seemingly explain why the country's criminal justice system's reoffending rate and prison numbers are so high. The prison population has increased by around 40,000 since 1993 from 44,246 to 85,134 (Webster, 2016). Young people are the most likely to reoffend post-custody, which currently stands at 70 per cent within 12 months of release, whilst for adults, it stands at almost 50 per cent (Prison Reform Trust, 2019).

The justice system trains professionals in risk-management, mental health, practice models, report writing and assessment skills but the most important skill is relationship building. I believe my hypothesis of the 'Risk Relationship Paradox' demonstrates that justice professionals also require continuous professional development in and supervision of relationship building. Although relationship is essential, unfortunately it gets little focus and it is possibly assumed that most professionals develop this skill over time. I believe this to be a real flaw in the system. Overcoming a lifetime of avoiding people that present risk, to building trusting relationships and human connections with them cannot be an easy transition, simply because you had a successful interview or obtained a degree in social work or youth justice. If changing something we have been conditioned to believe was easy is easy, the reoffending rate would be lower and we would have more success in changing those often conditioned to believe crime is acceptable. I might even be able to speak Spanish as well as my daughter. Restorative practice and trauma-informed practice go some way to developing this skill, but fall short of the targeted nature of examining how assessing risk of harm directly impacts on a relational space between service recipient and provider. Reflection is essential and service user involvement often provides discussions in the office that may not happen in the absence of those with lived experience. Just in the same way men wouldn't get it right talking about women in the absence of women.

I know through experience as a justice professional and recipient that being in the company of a justice professional through enforcement doesn't equate to connection. It doesn't allow the essential neural repetition required to influence significant change if the professional is not aware of the complexities of relational barriers. Attending an appointment through enforcement and feeling safe in a relationship to be receptive enough to a professional's advice and guidance are two very different things, especially when they are assessing you as *a risk*. The justice system at times conflates these two elements and this is one reason why I do not like the word 'engagement' or believe it's the most appropriate one for children in any context, as it implies sole responsibility to the child. There is a relationship *between the child and the system* and, to create equilibrium, that responsibility should be shared equally. This is something I have always naturally understood in my practice.

I spent lots of time with professionals as a recipient. I only remember those that were present enough to make me feel safe and unjudged (and with fondness that warms my heart even now). It was these professionals that I truly resonated with and accepted the information they provided which helped me along my transition to maturation. Even if I was not able to put what they told me into practice at that time due to developmental trauma, their information stayed with me like childhood memories of happiness. They were present and attuned to me relationally and the *feeling* is what I remember, not what they were telling me. The relationship first, information second. In the words of Van Der Kolk (2015),

> 'social support is not the same as merely being in the presence of others. The critical issue is reciprocity: being truly heard and seen by the people around us, feeling that we are held in someone else's mind and heart.'

Criminal justice, substance misuse, social care or mental health. It doesn't matter the reason why we come into someone's life; it is connection that makes the difference. This is *limbic resonance* and is a key relational component with young people in trouble as we will explore further in later chapters. Limbic resonance is explained by Hillarie Cash (2011) in her article in *Psychology Today* as 'the energetic exchange that happens between two people who are interacting in a caring and safe relationship,' echoing Dr Bruce Perry's (2020) model in his neurosequential work as explained in his talk 'Regulate, Relate, Reason.' This is exactly what I was lacking when I was a recipient of the Cognitive Behavioural Therapy Course in HM Prison Lindholme which I mentioned in *Chapter 3*. Limbic resonance is imperative for professionals to transmit their knowledge to justice recipients. Recipients distrust professionals due to worries about sanctions or external controls; and justice professionals have to overcome Risk Relational Paradox to achieve limbic resonance. From my professional perspective, I have in fact been blessed to spend time with some professionals that have obtained that level of connection and observing them enhanced my own practice. A commonality in the professionals and managers that I have witnessed achieving limbic resonance is that they get alongside young people in a comfortable, natural, social space that blossoms into trust, just like a daffodil in spring.

The system itself

Another relational issue to consider is that in over a decade of working within the youth justice field I have spent as much time in meetings about children as with children themselves. Such meetings include Risk-management Panels, Safety and Wellbeing Panels, Vulnerability and Risk-management Panels, Child Looked After Reviews, Strategy Meetings, Referral Orders Panels, Youth Rehabilitation Panels, Personal Education Plan meetings, Education Health and Care Plan meetings, and who knows how many intervention reviews as well as court hearings. Of course, these meetings are important and have their place. However they also create more work, reports and assessments for professionals and can feel overwhelming or stressful. Nigel Richardson, the former Director of Children's Services in Leeds and someone I have always admired stated in a BBC Radio programme 'From Cradle to Care' (2019) that the children's social care service should return to 'more helping — less assessing.' This really captures my point and observations about youth justice becoming institutional and that its functions, albeit evidenced-based, have developed into a barrier to relationship building. Again, a part of the solution, and also a part of the problem.

This level of bureaucracy trains professionals how to navigate their professional system when those receiving it as a service recipient have to navigate the system in a very different way. Navigating this level of bureaucracy develops what we often call professional jargon and, in my view, this develops a language and relational disconnect between professionals and service recipients. The best justice practitioners I have seen first-hand are those that can navigate our system whilst simultaneously supporting the recipients to navigate theirs. The starting point from my perspective is understanding how things impact on young people and relational connections. There are of course professionals that are stronger in certain areas than others, but from a service recipient perspective we don't care much for process or jargon. We simply need relational human beings that recognise the negative impact this institutional approach of process and risk-management can have on the relational sphere. If not delivered in a trauma-sensitive or informed way, it can further compound feelings of inequality and oppression: described by Lisa Cherry as 'system trauma.'

Service meetings often lead to further assessments and plans which create more time spent away from the very people I thought I would be spending time with. Although they have their place, they also create a barrier to the relational space from a professional perspective, in my view. This is another example of how I believe we have institutionalised public services. Practitioners, whether from justice, social care, mental health, substance misuse or universal services that work with the disadvantaged need space to be relational for communities that need them. I am not entirely sure the approach of caseloads, processes, deadlines and various meetings provides that space, or whether it creates stressed professionals and a tendency for service recipients to feel they are being worked with by a *system*, which I believe is how it feels for many. This is something we must be careful of as stressed professionals are less likely to be relationally available human beings, which is exactly what vulnerable children and families need. I want to reiterate: I am not suggesting we do not have such meetings or have processes as they are essential. I am just not sure we have struck the right balance. Just an observation that some professionals will agree with and some not.

In my experience, justice or risk meetings explore young people's life events in detail but rarely how relationships themselves have shaped children's identities. Events certainly have an impact on children and their development; however, they rarely shape the child's brain structure or function in the way relationships or environment do in their developmental years. This is particularly true if they have relational support to mitigate or buffer the event, or if the event happened at a time when they were resilient enough to manage how they responded emotionally. Yet, when assessing young people in a youth justice context, we inevitably find out about the child's chronological life events, rather than their relational experiences as they developed. We read about the events, but less about the impact they may have had on this child's development at that age and stage. This is why young people often feel defined by the worst things that have happened to them and not who they are, the adversities they have overcome or who they aspire to be. This is an unfortunate unintended consequence of a risk-management lens. Even when we claim to be solution-focused or person-centred, the central premise is institutional risk-management processes; and the most effective justice practitioners in my experience reflect and recognise how these impact on interconnection.

If we accumulate various significant events which are often negative in a childhood, we are still only assessing a very small percentage of a child's potential positive and negative relational experiences. It took me ten years to reflect as an adult and understand the collection of relational experiences that shaped my developing identity as a child. I couldn't have understood the significance or influence of each relationship on my violent behaviour, impulsivity, lack of attention, affect regulation or relational problems as a child. I didn't know or understand developmental trauma in this relational context, so how on earth would any professional understand it that came into contact with me before I was sent to prison as a criminally exploited 17-year-old? I am not suggesting that they should have done so, just that the risk assessment tool clearly has limitations when it comes to specifically understanding the root causes of behaviour, so the subsequent plans inevitably have significant limitations.

If we can't accurately assess the root cause or causes of behaviour, we have to consider that we could be causing harm if we are too directive. We may be providing psycho-educational interventions which rely on the use of young people's pre-frontal cortex and yet their lives may be so challenging that this area of the brain is often not accessible to them — as they are stuck in survival mode. This is why there is such a link between school exclusion and offending. It is not that exclusion causes crime; it is that the child is perhaps letting school know about their childhood relationships through behaviour, making our educational system's response an experience of further rejection.

One problem with feeling rejected as a child is when we gravitate to others that have experienced rejection too, we are then told to stay away from them because they are often negative influences. This leads to a further sense of isolation because we have a shared experience that some don't understand. It is not just a school problem or youth justice problem; it is a social justice and community problem so it requires a community and social response which sits harmoniously alongside the institutional one we have developed.

The most significant relationships which shaped my identity both positively and negatively as a child didn't seem significant until I had pondered and reflected as an adult. The relationships in my household were unstable, unreliable and dangerous, which left me feeling unsafe throughout my childhood and increased the activation of my stress response systems. The home is the relational context in which children must feel safe if they are to recover or heal from trauma and harmful events which impact on their self-worth and behaviour. However, due to structural inequality, these families are living in high crime areas impacted by poverty and hardship which often means the home is where the threat lies. The threat can lie outside the house if safe relationships situated within the household mitigate the threat. Issues arise when the threat sits within the relational context, because then children adapt as survivors and these adaptations manifest into behaviour.

None of this was identified throughout my decade of experiencing the justice system. It wasn't viewed as significant or, if it was, I wasn't provided with a positive relational repetitive pattern of relating to a safe, calm-brained adult which might have mitigated against these experiences. It was instead a fragmented and inconsistent experience of passing from one institution or professional to the next which unfolded into me being described as disengaged or hard to reach, yet I still maintain the system was not relational enough to reach me. I had various case notes and assessments which I accessed when writing my first book; however, I base my practice on being present, attuned and connected to the young person because I know this is what I required to make me feel safe. The best justice practitioners I have observed are able to discuss this with young people in an open and honest way, making the young person feel they understand how services haven't always got it right for them and not just focusing on the young person's behaviour. This is being present and attuned.

When a young person has not responded well to such experiences, what is the most effective way to re-programme the brain? How do we help the young person want to change identity or behaviour during a critical moment in their development? This is the million pound question and one that I believe we know the answer to. The work of Dan Siegal explained in his video 'How Relationships Shape Us' (2017), Bruce Perry in his video 'Born for Love' (2016) and by others needs to be central to the principles and research within the development of youth justice services. I hope to see the political and institutional will to focus primarily on it. I am only an individual, regardless of how many years I have spent on both sides of the justice system. I am not saying risk-management is not effective, not essential for public protection or that we don't need the risk-management processes. Just that the best practitioners understand how best to utilise them, but present themselves as relational human beings before process. That we ensure young people and adults in trouble believe they are embedded in our thoughts, hearts and minds and that we are not just retrieving information from them to either use in an assessment of their risk of harm or to pass on to other agencies, which may be used in a harmful way against them. How while using such methods, we can create a belief in young people that we are there for them, not just to risk-assess and change them, which creates a directive approach that feels oppressive in the absence of relational connections.

A 'Beyond Youth Custody' report focused on engaging young people in resettlement post-custody explored relationships with justice professionals. They found that girls felt

> 'caring was demonstrated where staff were compassionate, offered emotional support, acknowledged the impact of earlier negative experiences and the previous failure of agencies to deal with them, and provided practical advice and support in response to the needs articulated by the girls themselves' (Bateman et al, 2013).

The young people clearly wanted the issues they had identified to be resolved which highlights the importance of their views in any assessment or plan being produced. Other well-respected researchers in the field of youth justice have found 'there is an emerging consensus in the research literature that positive relationships between staff and service users are crucial to establishing and maintaining the involvement of disadvantaged young people in programmes of support' (McNeill, 2006). The key themes here seem to be co-production and inclusion of the young people into practice whilst being present enough to ensure that the young people understand we recognise how they were failed in the context of community and service.

In Leeds, I have been lucky to develop professionally in a 'Restorative, Child Friendly City.' My work has been varied and included offering young people in care and criminal justice the chance to help shape service delivery by listening to how they feel we could improve for the next generation. This work has always been more effective in relationship building than when I have case managed risk, due to the dynamic of the relationship and requirements of me to risk-assess young people. This is very interesting if the emerging consensus is that relationships are clearly so important and risk-assessment is such a relational barrier. Evidence at least in my view that there is a discussion to be had about risk-management in youth justice and how it is applied.

Young people questioned in the 'Beyond Youth Custody' (Bateman et al, 2013) research disclosed what they thought was a good practitioner and who were not. They stated that practitioners who 'cared about them' were better than those that did not. In my experience of relationship building in a justice context, this is often a reflection of when the young person believes that the relationship is more than an intervention. We will see in *Chapter 6*, 'Joint Enterprise,' that using common interests and shared social perspectives can be inclusive and that perceived bias can become a barrier. In the absence of securing and harnessing young persons' attentions and awareness, they often feel like they are being processed through transitions, as did I. The justice practitioners that provide authentic support in a realistic way are the practitioners that get the best results when it comes to relationship building. The managers that are regularly attuned to the relational needs of young people in trouble often make the best relational managers. This should always be the primary focus for any justice practitioner becoming a manager, leader and role model for other justice practitioners. Not only how well they understand the risk-management processes, inspection frameworks or theory, because they often lead the service narrative.

The Risk Relational Paradox is important to understand within relationship building as young people are saying (above) that good practitioners 'care about them.' By definition, this implies that they feel some practitioners don't care about them or don't demonstrate compassion and understanding. This is critical to building trusting relationships with young people in trouble. Without connection, how do we create an environment where self-concept might change? Have we developed a justice structure that doesn't value what it can't measure? Even if that is the very mechanism required to have a successful justice system, i.e. relationships, human connection and trust. We have witnessed the justice system over the last century develop from one of punishment to one of rehabilitation. Can we assume that this risk culture can naturally develop into a relational culture? We have changed language but maintain risk-management as a central function, so this seems to me an interesting question? I am sure we can develop, however we need to understand relationship building within this complex space. We must understand, too, how many risk or assessment processes impact on practitioner's capacity to provide that nurturing relationship to young people. It's not an easy task to break down all the complex barriers and practitioners need the time and space to do so.

Dr Dan Siegal in his talk 'Presence, Parenting and the Planet' (2019) provides insights into universal findings of parenting to help children thrive as the 'Four Ss' — Seen, Sooth, Safe and Secure. From a youth justice perspective, I view this through the 'Seen' component. The ability to be able to see the young person and their subjective reality and not just their behaviour. He describes this as the young person having their inner mental state being seen by an adult who is caring for their child. 'Felt' by another person who knows you, feels you and connects on a level required to break down barriers. This is not about what happened to you or what you have done, but about how you feel and think about the world. When children disengage, it is often due to them not feeling seen by services or professionals in a personal space. They simply make the relationship irrelevant at best, or a risk at worst. As the principle of the youth justice system is currently 'Child First, Offender Second' (Case, 2015), relationships and connection should be the primary focus to ensure children are seen. We must find a way to measure the relational experiences of the young people in the same way we measure risk-management processes, otherwise how can we ensure outcomes truly improve?

Justice professionals must be able to put themselves forward as 'Human First, Justice Professional Second.' This requires some level of personal availability, not just professional boundaries. This is why I believe we need to take a moment to consider the impact of too many complex processes on practitioners. If we want emotionally available practitioners for vulnerable children facing chronic and accumulated adversity, the relationship needs to be embedded by the industry. Of course, each process is developed through research and evidence, however do we know how these evidence-based processes impact on professionals' availability? Do they reduce stress levels or increase availability and does this impact positively or negatively on the relational space?

When I was a young person in trouble, I needed a human being as much as I needed a process or referral. Professionals effectively absorb and redirect children's emotional harm caused by various factors and a manager's responsibility, in my view, is to help practitioners redirect their emotions of vicarious trauma. 'Vicarious' meaning the emotional residue of exposure due to working directly with individuals that have experienced trauma. This is where being a restorative and trauma-responsive organization is essential. A less process driven industry with human connection as its primary function would be a trauma-responsive justice industry in my eyes. Relationally led organizations create safer spaces and would, I truly believe, be more effective in overall risk-management. I accept that this becomes far more difficult to regulate through inspection, but is a task we should take on nonetheless. In *Chapter 6*, Atticus discusses how he feels relationships even improve risk-management processes due to more information being shared with the practitioner as a result of being 'felt' and having a shared relational space.

Young people in the findings of the 'Beyond Youth Custody' (Bateman et al, 2013) research described certain qualities that they would expect to see from a practitioner that they believed 'cared' about them. These included demonstrating empathy, a non-judgemental attitude, conveying warmth and a readiness to go that extra mile. This clearly describes those practitioners that are able to connect on an emotional level and whom they believe have the time to go the extra mile. Those practitioners that are able to *see* them and look beyond their behaviour and stay attuned to them in an emotional and compassionate way. Being available for them while managing caseloads, processes and deadlines is no easy feat for practitioners working with this group. In my observations, the best practitioners are those that understand processes are important, however the relationship and being attuned to young people's needs is what creates a space for two humans to interconnect. The practitioners that strike the right balance between the perceptions of the young person and the requirements of the system and recognise that at times these elements do not complement each other.

Further thoughts on best practice

Best practice happens when practitioners recognise the disparity of power an institutional structure creates and work as hard as we can to assess issues with children as collaboratively as possible, otherwise we are likely to place further pressure on the young person. This does not mean tokenistically asking for the young person's views and filtering these into an academic assessment tool that they couldn't understand if they tried. It is about creating a plan that they have been actively involved in from start to finish. If not, we are simply using their views in a way that suits the system, instead of taking a journey with them and upskilling them as we take that voyage together. This requires justice practitioners that are restorative and trauma-informed in their practice and who recognise the Risk Relational Paradox. Exploring ways to resolve issues and conflict by being inclusive and allowing us to be led by those involved. Not so easy when we are managing the risk that someone possesses to be led by them, however it's imperative and makes the young people feel *seen* and *valued*. Treating someone as an expert in their experience will help develop connection and the relationship required to secure positive outcomes as identified by the young people themselves.

Without connection or trust, the young person may as well be a computer without the required software programme to receive and process the information we are sending. I feel that we have placed far too much emphasis on the content of programmes and not enough on who is delivering them and how. I think it would be useful to be recruiting and training those with lived experience of such programmes to assist in the delivery or co-production of the programmes. This would:

- Build on restorative practice and develop inclusion;
- Offer the opportunity to co-produce the style of delivery which means it is more likely to be appropriately received and therefore effective;
- Demonstrate that the justice system believes in redemption in a practical way;
- Mean the youth justice system is offering tangible examples of change;
- At the same time capitalise on skills this group have developed and provide employment opportunities that reduce the risk of reoffending.

'Beyond Youth Custody' (Ibid) also identified significant barriers that can impede the engagement of marginalised service users. These are

'frequently exacerbated in the case of young people in conflict with the law who have extensive, often negative, previous experience of criminal justice agencies.'

I would go beyond justice agencies. Many have experienced separation and loss after being removed from their families by children's social care, together with school exclusion. These experiences of school exclusion and removal from my family as a child damaged my own view of professionals. It meant that, when I came into contact with justice professionals, they needed to go the extra mile to make me believe they were there for me, not just for employment. This comes through nurturing the child in a way that makes them feel heard, felt, seen and accompanied through their journey of adversity. If we are not collaborative, restorative and inclusive in our approach, it can be perceived as if we are telling them we know how to navigate their experiences. The truth is, we don't. We only know how to build a rapport with them so we are in the best position to support them on their journey.

Challenges on multiple levels

Yes, this can of course be a challenge with this group on multiple levels—especially when the behaviours are extreme and the young person does everything in their power to replicate old patterns of relating, anticipating we won't step up and we won't be consistent or empathic or show we care. It could be because this way of working means we have to buy into restorative practice principles; we are here to do a job in the criminal justice system, not to make friends, so we may need to very skilfully balance high support *and* at times high challenge. It could challenge us as individuals within a much greater system, to think about our professional boundaries and how much we 'give' of ourselves. Nonetheless, the system itself is challenging enough, the last thing children that have experienced relational poverty, abuse, rejection and marginalisation need is further judgement from us for behaviours they simply don't have the capacity to understand or change without consistent nurturing support.

Naomi Thompson (2019) examined the current prevention measures in the UK which are designed to deter and prevent young people from being involved in organized crime. The research found challenges in defining organized crime, but interestingly that only one per cent of this type of crime involves under 18s. This highlights that young people are rarely orchestrators of serious crime; however, they are of course more likely to be exploited by others as opposed to exploiting others as we have already explored in earlier chapters. Thompson asks whether young people need to be a focus within organized crime strategy at all as they make up such a small proportion of this group. It also needs to be recognised that, often, the so-called perpetrators of exploitation were once young people, often also exploited. They have often experienced relationships themselves that shaped their identity. I believe this to be the cycle of abuse through interconnected community relationships.

I will explain in the next chapter that I call this the 'Risk Switch.' The lens through which services shift from a child being vulnerable to the risk *from* others, to seeing a young person, adolescent or young adult as being a risk *to* others. I first coined this term in my TEDx talk 'How Love Defeats Adversity' (Brierley, 2019). A complexity to this issue is how to keep children safe whilst simultaneously not alienating their attachments and older peers in a way that harms marginalised communities and our relationship with the child. These experiences or cycles rarely operate in a vacuum. These issues are relational and community-based and so this is how we should shape service responses. We certainly as individual practitioners do not want young people to believe we think negatively about their entire relational environment and networks as this will likely be an ineffective method of engagement. I thought this was a real push away from services when I perceived this is how my world was viewed by practitioners.

Within Thompson's research is cited the focus on relationship-based practice with the opportunity for long-term support from a key worker for young people who are vulnerable to involvement with crime as found by (Creaney, 2014). This is essential, not just for relationship building but also for understanding the life journey of the young person. If relationship-based practice is a primary focus of the youth justice system, I am surprised we have had little discussion about how to build and secure that relationship. My concern here is that using terms like 'disengagement' and 'hard to reach' is laying blame at the feet of those already facing severe hardship and adversity in society. If we have not been able to offer long-term relationship-based practice for a young person in trouble, haven't we as safeguarding service providers been hard to reach for them? It is important to listen to the voices of the three young people that are interviewed in *Chapter 6* to better understand what is most likely to secure that connection or relationship.

While we use terms like 'what works' within institutions such as criminal justice and children's social care, I am not sure this is the view of disadvantaged communities, through experience. The prison population has risen by 69 per cent in the last 30 years (Prison Reform Trust, 2019), children in care numbers have increased decade after decade since 1994 (Department of Education, 2017) whilst new research shows that the number of children entering care within a week of birth almost doubled between 2007/8 and 2017/18 (Bilson, 2020). The root causes of this are far to complex for me to identify here and I will not attempt to claim to know the answer. However, there is either something wrong with how society is structured for the most vulnerable, or how we are delivering services to the most disadvantaged communities, or both. Our default position may be to label vulnerable members of communities that we have left behind as hard to reach, when in fact the way we deliver services may not meet their relational needs, or may even make their lives harder.

If the child, as Dr Bruce Perry (2016) states, requires repetitive human interactions to develop empathy, compassion, patience or trust, it would seem that relational experiences and not programmes would be the most effective way to develop such skills. It highlights that it is not that young people in trouble don't take responsibility. It is often that they haven't learnt how to and we are likely compounding their experience if we do not provide a safe, consistent community context from which to heal or develop new skills and ways of thinking. These skills can only be developed within their own community. Furthermore, maybe creating spaces for those children most at risk of developing behaviours in their early years is a far better investment for the taxpayer than institutions and professionals with a bias to claim to know what works, even in the face of the raw statistics evidencing otherwise.

Dr Ross Greene (2010) is a child psychologist and author who maintains, 'Kids do well when they can,' and when they can't it's because they are delayed in the development of crucial cognitive skills. He argues that when working with challenging young people our philosophy guides our actions. I share his philosophy that kids do well if they can, and recognise also that social and relational factors can hold them back. This is what I experienced throughout my development growing-up too. I would get released from custody and return to the exact same relational context which had played a significant role in my incarceration in the first place. I was never released to a change in environment which highlights shortcomings in the incarceration process and 20-minute appointments with probation which was the intervention that works according to research. Yet, I would argue, and others are entitled to disagree, that in various ways, this intervention caused as much harm to my reoffending as it did good and this is something we must discuss if we want to be effective.

I was trying to 'do well' and found it incredibly challenging due to exposure to traumatic relational factors preventing me from doing so. This caused internal pain and self-rejection which led to addiction and subsequently offending. I received very little relational input from the youth justice system to help reshape my identity positively after it had been shaped negatively by relationships throughout development and subsequently by incarceration. I am not arguing against incarceration, or for it, just that it can compound the self-perception of young people being alien to everyone else. Therefore, it is our responsibility as justice professionals to believe in children and inspire them wherever possible. It can be a challenge, however it is best done by those that believe the child will do well if they can and gives the right relational support. If they return to past behaviours it is often because they are seeking safety within familiar relationships, even at a cost of their authenticity, because they, like everyone else, are led by their attachment needs.

In any sense, young people and crime is never a straightforward concept as we have found. Thompson (2019) stated there is a 'blurred line between the young person as criminal or as exploited, and for interventions to view prevention of crime and protection or safeguarding of young people as overlapping.' Others such as Case and Haines (2015) found the Positive Youth Justice approach offers a model that draws on these elements and that could be translated from a post-offending to a preventive intervention. Again, focusing on the community and family factors strongly associated with youth crime, not the symptoms of it. There is a consistent theme of young people that enter the criminal justice system being shaped by social and relational factors.

Effective practice therefore should be sought in relational and community spaces. Role models and mentors with similar life experience or justice experience that the young people view as authentic should be considered. The youth justice system has been incredibly successful over recent years in reducing the number of young people coming into contact with the system altogether.

'The number of first-time entrants has fallen by 85 per cent since the year ending March 2009, with an 18 per cent fall since the year ending March 2018 [and] the number of children who received a caution or sentence has fallen by 83 per cent over the last ten years, with a 19 per cent fall in the last year' (Youth Justice Board, 2018/2019).

Avoiding the cycle of abuse

It is great that we have acknowledged that criminalising children is counter-productive for children to grow and have crime-free lives or better outcomes. However, we must explore the increase, decrease and what happened to firstly criminalise so many young people and what caused the more recent reduction.

The Ministry of Justice Analysis (MOJ, 2017, p. 4) concluded that,

'Changes in policing practices appear to be the most likely (but probably not the only) driver of both the increase and then the decrease in the number of First Time Entrants (FTEs) in England and Wales between 2003/04 and 2012/13. Specifically, the introduction of the Offences Brought to Justice (OBTJ) target appears to have led to a sharp increase in the number of young people brought into the formal youth justice system for the first time. This in turn led to shifts in the characteristics of FTEs, with greater volumes of low-seriousness offences being formally sanctioned.'

Although in the same report, the MOJ states that crime overall has dropped and therefore other factors are likely to have played a role in the reduction of FTEs, the one thing that cannot be overlooked is that while FTEs have reduced significantly over the past decade, according to the YJB (2017/18, p. 36) the child incarceration rate 'shows large falls of 70 per cent over the last 10 years.' Taylor was therefore correct in that early contact with the justice system increases reoffending and an escalation of children and young people through the system itself, often due to breach of orders and reoffending leaving the courts limited options. The question is why when the youth justice system is not primarily a punitive one and youth justice staff are in the main child friendly and understand their needs. I believe Risk Relational Paradox plays a significant role.

The justice system as already highlighted conflates enforced attendance with human connection. However, as Dr Perry points out, the only way to reshape a child's identity and behaviour is through repetition from someone that the child believes can regulate them, relate to them, so together they can reason. This is only likely to happen in a trusting relationship, not one that is forced, or a relationship the child or young person doesn't perceive to be more than an intervention. If:

- we are able to get the relational experience right by recognising that these young people are often products of their environments and that we as justice professionals are the key holders to change as much as any research or programme, we can and will get better results;
- our philosophy is right and our connections are authentic, the young people will be receptive to our information;
- we are led by risk-management process and inspection frameworks, the child and possibly the availability of professionals to be present will get lost in the industrial mechanism.

It doesn't mean we will get the results straightaway, or that it will be easy. However, we will find a place in their hearts and, although we may not be able to measure that, believe me when I say this, that is enough to make a difference. Let's explore what happens when we do not get it right and the many children we once deemed vulnerable become influencers to other young people through a cycle of abuse.

CHAPTER 5

The Risk Switch

Two of the most pressing recent issues for the youth justice system and other services that work with vulnerable young people in the UK is to tackle county lines and child criminal exploitation. Before we go on to discuss each of these in any detail, these are the Government's own definitions:

'County lines is a term used to describe gangs and organized criminal networks involved in exporting illegal drugs into one or more importing areas within the UK, using dedicated mobile phone lines or other forms of "deal line". They are likely to exploit children and vulnerable adults to move and store the drugs and money and they will often use coercion, intimidation, violence (including sexual violence) and weapons.' (Home Office, 2020).

'Child Criminal Exploitation is common in county lines and occurs where an individual or group takes advantage of an imbalance of power to coerce, control, manipulate or deceive a child or young person under the age of 18. The victim may have been criminally exploited even if the activity appears consensual. Child Criminal Exploitation does not always involve physical contact; it can also occur through the use of technology. Criminal exploitation of children is broader than just county lines, and includes for instance children forced to work on cannabis farms or to commit theft.' (Ibid).

Carlene Firmin (2019) in her TEDx Talk 'Contextual Safeguarding: Rewriting the Rules of Child Protection,' highlighted that we believe we have done quite well here in the UK in terms of child exploitation. Explaining that as we have now defined child criminal and sexual exploitation, knife crime and youth crime as child abuse, she also explains that although this is, of course, progress we shouldn't assume that simply identifying these concepts as child abuse means the systems designed to deal with it know how to respond. I agree with her entirely and also her statement that child protection services need to work with a wealth of social actors within communities to create an appropriate and measured responses to exploitation.

Reflecting on writing my first book, it dawned on me that my community (or 'village') didn't intervene in what was clearly adult dealing, exploitation and taking advantage of a vulnerable family. If statutory services such as the police, social care, probation or youth justice are not viewed as protectors against the toxic environments within villages, the average person in those villages will not want to get involved due to the consequences of doing so. We can, in my view, challenge that notion by employing and recruiting those that have recovered from such experiences that understand these villages from the inside out. This will also improve the interface or 'disconnect' between communities and authority. The best way to keep children safe from those within a village is to become a part or an extension of the village itself.

Young people being exploited criminally is not a new phenomenon by any means. It is just a slight switch in the lens through which services view children involved in offending. The issues have reached mainstream media and politicians alike which has resulted in services currently shaping their approaches to keep children safe from being exploited into crime by older peers. This has resulted in various measures, including relationship disruption, children in care being moved into placements (sometimes in other cities or towns) to keep them safe and children even being secured under section 25 of the Children Act 1989 (legislation that allows children to have their liberty removed to keep them safe from themselves or others). These look like responses that may protect in the short-term, but what are the long-term harms these measures can have on communities and children?

More on child exploitation

In my view, exploitation is just the start of a conversation that is taking us in the right direction, but we are still very early in our understanding of the relational process which leads children to be persistently or seriously involved in crime. Children have been criminally exploited since the dawn of time. Just think about Charles Dickens' Victorian novel *Oliver Twist* as filmed many times but originally written in serial form for newspapers from 1827–1839. Although fictional, the message was staring us in the face. Sometimes, we develop our service responses far too late. Children being exploited criminally shouldn't come as any surprise. Throughout our journey in this book, we have discovered that children's brains and minds develop through their own lived experience, environment and relationships. Therefore, when we learn of any child heavily involved in crime, we should be curious about whether something is or was wrong with their relational experiences throughout their development. Instead of assessing life events, we should recognise that it is often consistent exposure to relationships or environments that construct an identity which leaves children like I was at risk of exploitation. Exploitation is often an evolving relational process, and rarely just a singular event.

Exploitation was part of the reason I wanted to write *Your Honour Can I Tell You My Story?* I was already well on a road to criminality and addiction, way before I was coerced into selling heroin by adult drug dealers. They took full control of my family's home when I was only 15, after I experienced school exclusion, the care experience and exposure to consistent criminal relationships which I call 'relational criminality.' Almost every adult male that took the place of my absent father was involved in crime, or at least took drugs frequently and had a mistrust of authority, so when my older adult peers offered me the chance to spend time with them it made complete sense at that time. I was consequently sentenced to two 18 months long prison terms for selling their drugs and making them considerable amounts of money, while I developed a toxic heroin addiction. The adults that provided me with drugs never faced justice, regardless of the wealth of evidence the police had that the drugs didn't belong to me or my family.

This evidence included me being arrested as a passenger in one of their high-performance cars. My family had nothing of value in the family home except a lot of Class A drugs at the time it was searched. There is no doubt that when this happened, in 1998, and for decades before then, children have been groomed due to their vulnerability and then punished by the justice system for being coerced into crime. This is one of many examples of how institutions can unintentionally compound the adversity of those who have already faced significant harm by a social structure they had little to no influence in constructing. This is how structural inequality works for some of our most vulnerable children when they are punished for surviving chronic levels of adversity. These issues disproportionately affect disadvantaged communities, especially children in trouble that eventually face incarceration.

It is a complex relational journey to become a child that is unable to recognise risk in the way I couldn't, so it needs a complex understanding of the issue to know how to respond. I am not sure an institutional response of assessments and risk-management processes is always going to be most effective. The African saying, 'It takes a village to raise I child' (*Chapter 2*) doesn't mean a professional with a clipboard, assessment questionnaires and national standards. This is institutionalised services in my view, not extended village members. Not that these institutional processes are unimportant, just that they affect the relational experience from the young person's perspective. The best justice practitioners I believe are those that understand this effect and mitigate this through their relationships.

If we view exploitation through the lens of interconnected relationships and shared identity, we can start to have a nuanced discussion about the most effective ways to respond. As defined above, county lines is a more targeted element of exploitation in which groups or organized gangs specifically approach children or vulnerable adults with the primary aim of them selling drugs to reduce the likelihood of gangs or those further up the supply chain being caught or losing money themselves. Exploitation, in a criminal sense, has an association with *relational poverty* (Perry, 2012; Lawson et al, 2018) which is best explained by patterns of human relationships. The correlation is the inability to access positive or pro-social relationships due to having a specific social or family identity within a community. As relationships are a reciprocal process, children alone don't get to choose their social relationships, as we have already explored. If they experience social marginalisation, they will naturally gravitate towards others that they perceive to be part of their in-group and those they feel comfortable with, as is true for us all. These relationships are likely to cross age, capacity and maturity sets. They are likely to be natural evolutionary relationships and not necessarily targeting of those we perceive as vulnerable victims due to a lower age. As exploitation is such a complicated relational process, we need to consider our response, and not compound the experience of inequality and social marginalisation of a group already disproportionately affected.

Robert Merton's *Strain Theory* (1938) explained how an inability to access the American Dream or middle-class status influenced criminality. Back in the 1930s, he of course didn't consider intergenerational trauma, ACEs or relational poverty. He certainly didn't consider the impact of exploitation through a relational lens. He explained criminality through the lens of material inequality within a consumerist, capitalist system and the inability of the disadvantaged to obtain a respectable social status; however, this doesn't explain deviant or anti-social crime which accounts for vast amounts of youth crime. He was not exploring the relationships people involved in offending have with the State or authority. A child stating that 'professionals only work with me because they are paid to do so,' speaks volumes about the relational lens through which they are seeing the world. Many see a bleak future for themselves which creates a connection with older peers that also have poor outcomes. Most young people heavily involved in offending make very little financial gain through their criminal behaviour, suggesting that Merton's theory was way off the mark in exploring child criminal exploitation. This is important because theories such as his shape the lens in which we see crime today.

The need for attachment and relationships

Let's for a moment imagine the world through the eyes of a young person who has very limited access to pro-social relationships due to their experience of relational poverty. Now imagine how they feel when authority figures that they often have a complex relationship with seek to disrupt those relationships because they are assessed as negative, due to their friends being older and involved in anti-social behaviour. However, building relationships with peers who have the same or similar experiences is an unfortunate reality of the lives of many young people in trouble, so we really have to think about how we respond as authority figures. Just as in the same way we have come to realise that removing children from birth families can have profound negative consequences, even if the parents' behaviours are harmful, because attachment is a primary human need.

Teenagers need attachments just as much as young children do and Dr Gabor Mate (2011) as well as Dr Dan Siegal (2014) argue that, in adolescence, teenagers require attachments to peers as a survival need. It is a developmental phase which requires young people at this stage to understand they are becoming less dependent on parents or carers and therefore need to build attachments to other 'village mates.' Therefore, severing them will have profound consequences too. Furthermore, this approach is likely to compound the feeling of State control and inequality for the developing child or young person. It seems to me that, when we as an authority save the vulnerable, it always comes at a cost for other vulnerable members of the village yet we write the narrative making us the heroes.

Child criminal exploitation often, albeit not always, involves young people spending time with older peers that are involved in crime or have poor outcomes. As a result, they themselves are offered the opportunity to offend or be involved in drug and alcohol use, which they often accept because they are crying out for a sense of belonging or attachment to a group that they feel comfortable in. We will explore some personal examples of this in the next chapter, 'Joint Enterprise.' The social interaction, albeit not positive, is often developed because of relational poverty and with people that fall within their 'in-group' or perceived like-minded people. Many have shared experiences of marginalisation by the very institutions that are responsible for social inclusion such as education. They are often criminalised by the police early in their lives which reinforces their identity or self-perception as outsiders. Then, as a result of all the rejection from their *village*, they gravitate towards other marginalised peers, often believing they are the ones doing the rejecting, to save face or feel better about the perceived rejection. They will then create a subjective reality that they are fighting a system that is out to get them. This means our response needs to be extremely well thought through, measured and inclusive. Otherwise we could cause more harm and intensify the feeling of inequality instead of improving outcomes or reducing victims which is the function of the justice system.

The wonderful lived experience educator and author of the foreword to this book, Lisa Cherry (2020) wrote an article about this during the midst of the Covid-19 crisis. Lisa explains that the social or physical distancing we are all experiencing while out walking is something that 'many people face every single day. This includes those that experience racism, care, mental health or addiction.' The vast bulk of those that end up within the youth justice system often experience intersectionality of detrimental social factors throughout their development as children. Children like I was understand this is happening, disconnect and find social groups they feel safer with and more accepted in. Of course, this sense of connection is often found in unsafe relationships, but at least they are not relationships based on processes such as assessments, plans, interventions or referrals to other professionals that are paid to 'fix' youngsters. However, as a society, we blame and demonise older peers because they are an easy target. Not fully-recognising the complex factors leading to the relational connections. Notwithstanding, the fact that these older peers were often vulnerable children that once faced the very same experiences in their childhoods highlights the importance of an inclusive community approach based on collaboration and not exclusion or demonisation.

Dan Siegal, in his 2nd edition of *The Developing Mind* (2015, p. 15) explains how our 'social experiences can directly shape our neurological architecture.' As our neurological pathways shape our identity and who we feel comfortable around or identify with, disrupting the relational connections with others by the establishment that played a role in them coming together may cause more long-term harm than good. Severing relationships that are formed through a connection of trauma and social rejection is likely to compound the feeling of marginalisation and oppression. Although this is all done with the intention of protection and safeguarding, we could isolate children even further if we don't work together with and educate communities to develop relational buffers. Our authoritarian default mechanisms are usually perceived to be punitive by this social group. I am not arguing we do nothing of course. Just that we may miss the nuances around this sensitive discussion and an individual approach by authority in the absence of community measures and inclusion may lead us to demonise people already tackling social exclusion.

Ineffective penal consequences

Naomi Thomson (2019) states that, overall, the literature she explored suggests that an approach to crime prevention through enforcement and a focus on penal consequences is ineffective. This is due to the systems at play working with children, families and communities in their silos. Such families experience services that are fragmented rather than working together, such as substance misuse, social care, education, criminal justice, public health and mental health. These families need a coordinated, relational response to support them, not a multitude of professionals within a complex multi-agency system. This approach also doesn't take into account that we are all interconnected and the only way to reduce these harms overall is working with communities, not individuals through enforcement. If we are not more inclusive with older peers, the younger children that are connected to them will also feel demonised, so our approach must be holistic and include, where possible, community members they can learn to trust.

An individual risk-management approach seems on the face of things to keep everyone safe; so why would the criminal justice system require reform if it is effective. Every new government expresses its view of the reforms required. Nick Herbert (2012), Minister of State for Policing and Criminal Justice, stated, 'The system is in need of modernisation, with old-fashioned and outdated infrastructures and ways of working that suit the system rather than the public it serves.' I interpret his words as referencing what I have already claimed to be an institutional response to what I believe are relational and community issues. If it is often a lack of relational support many in the justice system lack and require, we have to ask whether our institutional responses meet the relational needs of those that enter as recipients. I am convinced now more than I ever have been that the poor outcomes for both children's social care and the criminal justice system are because the simple answer on a societal level is, 'No we don't meet those needs.' Yet, because the disparity of power between the State and vulnerable communities is so vast, the level of individual accountability versus institutional accountability is also complex and vast.

I believe prisons and the criminal justice system have to integrate into early help services and stop viewing intergenerational issues as isolated incidents. Youth justice professionals need to deliver training around ACEs, intergenerational trauma and the harm caused when children develop a criminal identity within prisons to prisoners. Substance misuse agencies need to work in children's centres with fathers to address their issues so they can be present fathers, just a couple of examples. Human interaction is based on interconnectedness, so the best early help or prevention measure is treating every adult as the next potential parent, regardless of their behaviour. We manage risk to keep people safe, but what if overall the consequences of risk-management approaches negatively affect disadvantaged communities? In the words of Lisa Cherry (2020), 'We work with people as if adults have never been children, and children do not become adults.' This is something we need to change within services. We need to see adults with behavioural issues as assets who need support, not just adults who are a threat to children. Many have experienced turbulent childhoods and we at one time viewed them as vulnerable children too. We must always recognise the harm demonising older peers has on young people who believe they will grow-up to become just like their older peers. It is naive to fall into a trap of viewing ourselves as heroes, while simultaneously being considered adversaries to the communities these individuals are connected to.

What we know about the structure of the brain and neurobiology is that identity is developed in part by social experience and relationships. It is what connects us to others and desistance theory within criminology has identified changing identity as being a significant factor in helping people desist from offending and reoffending. Taking this into account, it explains how we are able to flip the risk from safeguarding the child or being a victim of circumstance to becoming a perpetrator or negative influencer of other vulnerable children. This is an intricate and complex process and requires more research to understand the statistics behind this reality, and whether we are achieving our objective of breaking this cycle of abuse or making things worse.

We pour billions of taxpayer's pounds into services such as criminal justice, social care, mental health and substance misuse which employ people who often live outside of poverty to help people living in poverty better cope while tackling poverty. This does not mean if you haven't experienced similar experiences you cannot or should not help. It does however mean we must avoid judgements or labels as much as possible as they are unhelpful and do not recognise the disparity of power or relational poverty many of those receiving public services experience.

Adults that influence their younger peers in a negative way were once children, often who had something happen along their journey which set them off course. Inclusion and open hearts are what people that have drifted away from society need to bring them back. A belief from those within that society that they belong just as much as anyone else, regardless of their functionality. This applies to those with care experience, homelessness, drug and alcohol issues, and yes, even criminality. Early intervention cannot exist in a vacuum. Offering me an opportunity and educating me was early intervention for my daughter and it happened a decade before she was even thought about. If we alienate and demonise young adults today, we must realise that they are tomorrow's parents. These issues are intergenerational, so the cycles don't start and finish, they just interconnect on a human level.

As already indicated, of every four adult prisoners you would meet in a prison, one would have spent time in the care system (Laming, 2016). The link between care and custody is a complex one which we will explore later when we examine that between trauma and youth crime. However, if one in four have been in care, it means many more would have had children's social work service involvement through being a child in need or child protection interventions. Most social care interventions don't result in removal of children, so one can only imagine that the number is much higher than one in four, however this data is almost impossible to extrapolate for various reasons. Having reflected on my personal journey through the fragmented services in education, children's social work services and adult services (including the prison system and probation) it makes me wonder how many others experienced this transition. I have put together a diagram to visually explain the process.

The 'Risk Switch' in the form of a diagram

I call this 'The Risk Switch.' The diagram explains how children born into a predisposition of intersectional challenges which impact on attuned, nurturing relationships such as poverty, abuse and neglect often see this passed down intergenerationally from parent to child. Parental mental health can include exposure to criminality. Relational criminality is not always parental, however. Often it can be familial relationships in what should be safe spaces or with adults within the home environment. The ACEs are as defined by Felitti et al (1998), social rejection, discrimination and racism. When this is the case, the child is often deemed vulnerable and needs protecting by services so they are shielded as much as possible from exposure to such factors. Services often do all they can, however, as already stated, as services are often fragmented into those for adults and children, criminal justice or mental health and substance misuse services, the early help services that truly understand this intersectional nature at birth do not follow that child through the life course. Leaving a story of the child being passed from professional to professional, service to service. This is often interpreted in different ways from different perspectives and used in different ways depending on service need, requirements and agendas.

RISK SWITCH DIAGRAM

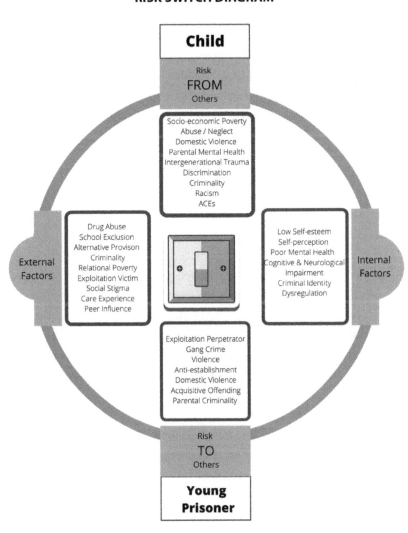

Children who for a variety of reasons are unable to manage the intersectional nature of such issues can develop internal and external challenges while evolving into adolescence. It is not due to them lacking resilience, character or internal strength. This is in fact a damaging misinterpretation in my experience and according to expert theory and developing science (Shankoff, 2007 p. 11). Shonkoff states the central feature of toxic stress is the absence of supportive adults to help the child cope.

In my care files, it states I was the first child to return home post-care as I was the 'most resilient' of all five children. All five failed to complete school and had drug and alcohol issues during adolescence. Suggesting that a high dosage of adversity in the absence of attuned adult relationships was the most significant factor to toxic stress developing into poor social outcomes. We are born with in innate potential of resilience and attachment but it requires nurturing relationships or experience to develop (Siegal, 2017). Some young people may at a later stage have access to the relationships or stability required to overcome the original difficulties at birth. This was established in the conclusions of Hambrick, et al (2018) when they explored the timing of childhood adversity. They found that 'even if a child's early experiences are poor, improving future relational contexts will likely improve outcome.' But what if they do not and the nature of adversity continues in the absence of supportive, nurturing relationships into adolescence?

If we were unable to, or did not provide human connections that develop the potential that all children have for attachment and resilience, child criminal exploitation can swiftly switch the lens we see the young person through. They can travel through a service lens from the child that was at risk *from* others, to an individual that is a risk *to* others (Brierley, 2019). The labels of perpetrator, criminal, exploiter or offender then make the maturation or desistance process more difficult and prolonged. It can also compound the relationship between the individual and authority; many already feel failed due to not being protected from harm in the first place. First, the Risk Switch diagram allows justice practitioners to recognise the life challenges many persistent young people and adults have had during the very years of developing identity and group membership. Second, it allows us to respond with the compassion, understanding and authenticity required to build a relationship most likely to effect change. This is where the language of 'What happened to you?' instead of 'What have you done?' becomes so important as we will explore in *Chapter 7*, 'Youth Crime and Trauma.' If the individual believes we see their pain, we will be more likely to be a part of the healing.

The Risk Switch was the process I experienced as a child born to a care leaving mother and also something I don't believe we talk about enough, especially when I hear the rhetoric about older peers exploiting young people. I transitioned through a Risk Switch within the lens of services. However, I experienced no conscious transition at all. It was an organic sequence of events and relationships which services couldn't have understood, as their approach was everything but relational or sequential. It felt to me that each professional I came into contact with was more interested in their intervention being effective than being in my life long enough or with enough consistency to make a significant difference. It seemed they were far too busy assessing my risk or managing cases to become the relational buffer I needed to mitigate the relational harm I was exposed to throughout the transition. Some justice professionals were able to manage the stresses behind the scenes and have a relationship with me. They all had vary-ing levels of ability to connect with me which, I believe, was their capacity to personally connect with someone with my background or behaviour through the Risk Relational Paradox context.

In my years of working within youth justice, many children and young people have been themselves victims of criminal exploitation and then tran-sitioned to so called perpetrators after they left children's services and became young adults. Their needs are often lost because they are now viewed as those that harm children and no longer the child that was harmed. The term 'Risk Switch' as demonstrated in the diagram is something I believe is critical when we explore child criminal exploitation and how children view the relationships their peers or perpetrators have with authority. This is because I view exploita-tion through the lens of interconnected relationships, but also through identity. We need far more research into the effectiveness of the youth justice system not only diverting the most prolific and serious young people away from offending and, as a result, how many of these young people are known to be involved in shaping the identity of other young people they are in contact with as they develop. It is difficult to expect children to make safe choices if their brain structure and function is being shaped by their peer relationships within com-munities shaped by adults.

By the age of 15, I was more scared of the police and authorities than violent drug dealers, partly due to my behaviour but also partly due to my life experiences teaching me that services couldn't keep me from the harm in my community. We have recognised exploitation more now than when I was a child, but have we developed trust between such young people and services and, if we haven't, what will the long-term effects of disrupting their peer relationships be? Are we more likely to disrupt the trust they have with authority and are we creating a short-term fix to what is often a long-term relational issue? For me the switch took place several years after services failed to protect me and my siblings from a toxic exposure to adversity and criminality. This shaping of my identity was the most significant contributing factor as to why I was exploited in later years. It also affected my general relational experiences and ability to sustain school or identify with or trust professionals. Adults I identified with through development taught me I could not to trust authority and my experience was the authorities couldn't protect children like me anyway.

This was my own implicit bias (created by my social and relational experiences), i.e. that anyone in a position of authority couldn't keep me safe and therefore couldn't be relied upon. I consequently needed to create my own way of surviving the world I perceived as dangerous. I would argue my exploitation process started years before I was actually provided with drugs by an adult to sell on. Almost all the adults that I came into contact with committed crime in one way or another. Given adults shape the children in their care, maybe the definition of exploitation needs expanding to include when adults expose children to criminality as this is through their position of power in the relationship. Maybe this would shape prevention services in a criminal justice context.

I think I have presented enough evidence to start this discussion. If not, please explore the work of Tzoumakis (2017) who found that a parental history of severe criminal offending increased the risk of high levels of aggression in offspring during early childhood, highlighting the need for intervention with families during this key developmental period. As we have already explored, children are resilient and will develop strategies to tackle their environments and attach to adults and subsequently peers to survive. We invest so much in changing their identities or marginalising them as adults when, surely, it's cheaper and safer for those children if we prevent the identity developing in the first place.

The relationships I was able to access were limited and older peers with similar experiences were available; so, I think we tried unsuccessfully to buffer each other's experiences of trauma and harm. Dan Siegal in his 2nd edn of *The Developing Mind* (2015, p. 165) when discussing mirror neurons explains that 'the mirror neuron system learns from experience.' Which also explains why Andrew in the next chapter doesn't view himself as a victim of exploitation, even as an adult who has changed his behaviour and desisted from offending. As a child, he secured relationships with adults he felt connected to and the consequence was that the State placed him in custody. He then received financial and interconnected relational support from the adults who were thought to have exploited him while being punished through incarceration by the State. The same State that now claims he was exploited by those adults who supported him while he was incarcerated by the State. These are some of the complexities, nuances and intricate dynamics we have to explore if we are to seriously reduce the development of criminal identities we later want to change. Defining it has highlighted a generation of youth and criminal justice failings but, as Carlene Firmin asks, does that mean child protection services know how to prevent it? Children's experiences haven't changed as much as we would like to believe; sadly, for many, as exploitation is exactly what I and others I know experienced in 1998.

The definition of child criminal exploitation as a result of this science, theory and insight seems far too simple, even for those of us that have fallen victim to the process. It seems to me to be a way of again individualising a social issue and placing blame on those older peers that have also faced severe hardship. Relational poverty seems to me to be the root cause of so many issues including exploitation of children and the development of identity through social interaction. Now we have identified the issues, we should recognise that the response needs to sit within communities. A divide and conquer response may seem like safeguarding the child on an individual level, however we should also be asking why we weren't keeping them safe in the first place and why they view us as services as a risk. Safeguarding services have been working with these children, families and communities throughout years of this exploitation, so why were we unable to firstly identify it and, also, why don't these vulnerable families and communities trust services to protect them. My view is that the Risk Switch plays a role because children have never operated in isolation and seek attachments. If services are demonising the adults they attach to, we effectively demonise the child through their lens.

There are similarities between criminal and sexual exploitation, but there are also significant differences. We seem to conflate them due to the label 'exploitation.' Identity is the key factor for child criminal exploitation and that identity often starts way before any exploitation takes place through the relational experience, throughout development. We need to consider the shaping of criminal identities and then think about what we can do to disrupt this process before it begins and accountability for services if the switch happens before the brain has matured around the age of 24. Early help services need to consider the development of criminal identities and work closely with criminal justice organizations, and even prisons and prisoners, and not view them through an adversarial risk-management lens.

I delivered a workshop in HM Prison Leeds in 2019 to 50 prisoners around ACEs and the prisoners received the information well. Maybe we should train prisoners in better understanding developmental trauma, to be facilitated by ex-prisoners so they can be the change makers upon release in their own communities. Maybe we can work together so they can be assets, not just risks to their children and their communities. We should be bringing people together, using collaborative services that understand these individuals and communities.

Relational criminality seems to explain why we are seeing more children looked after that are removed in their teenage years coming into contact with the justice system. HM Prisons and Probation Service's 'Care Leavers in Prison and Probation' (2019) found that 'maltreatment and going into care as a teenager may be more strongly associated with youth offending than maltreatment or care only.' It's not that children of this age shouldn't be removed if they are not safe or, of course, the parents are not able to safely parent, it's just that I'm concerned with the disruption of human connection at the adolescent stage of development within marginalised groups. Even if the relationship is viewed as negative by the local authority. Can this disruption cause as much damage as the relationship itself? Local authorities need to assist in building stronger relational networks in communities, rather than trying to co-parent children who are often programmed to not recognise their authority, let alone view them as parents. This simply increases their risk of so many vulnerabilities, including running back into the arms of what they perceive to be safe and familiar relationships and away from fear.

I have worked as a professional between the justice and care system for several years as a specialist and my experience aligns with the findings of HMPPS above. That most of the children looked after who enter custody are often those that enter care in adolescence or for short periods. They often also continue to have contact, both supervised or not, with families who present with the same risk factors as the young people who enter the youth justice system (Youth Justice Board, 2015) who are not care experienced. This would indicate that care itself is certainly not a causal link, but just a shared experience. As stated previously, we often do not find out about offending within the families or extended networks of children that offend because, unless it has resulted in a conviction, the family are incredibly unlikely to make services aware of any criminality. Or, as with me as a child, services may be aware, but are limited in ensuring it doesn't shape a child developing an identity that leaves them vulnerable to exploitation.

Care may at times compound a child's negative early life experiences due to experiences of separation and detachment. However, it's more likely that the common factors they share with non-looked after children in custody is developmental trauma and relational criminality which have shaped their identity and social group membership explaining Laming's (2016) findings that 94 per cent of children looked after do not come into contact with the youth justice system.

Bessel Van Der Kolk (2015) explains that when it comes to victims of trauma, they can often gravitate towards each other with profound negative outcomes. He explains that they can

'focus on shared history of trauma and victimisation which alleviates their searing sense of isolation, but usually at the price of having to deny their individual differences. Members can belong only if they conform to the common code.'

Although exploitations may of course be negative for young people, they are often the only interpersonal experiences on offer for that child. Helping children develop strategies to manage such relationships would seem the most effective approach in assisting them to navigate what is often a turbulent environment. If these children don't trust us as services, then we need to question our approach. Otherwise, we are seemingly misusing our position of privilege by not recognising such day-to-day issues of survival. We should step into the dark room with them to bring them into the light, otherwise we may drag them out and make them fear the light altogether.

When Malcolm (not his real name) in my story exploited me aged 15, it was due to the fact that I didn't feel he represented any risk to me. During my early years, almost every adult male I had around in the absence of my biological father was involved in varying levels of criminality and violence. Yes, I knew he sold drugs and he was also known to be violent but our identities were interconnected through our inability to access positive alternative relationships and experiences of intersectionality. It was of course exploitation; however, it has to be viewed within a wider relational context of marginalisation. Carlene Firmin et al (2020) relate this to be a component of 'contextual safeguarding.' Even within a community riddled with poverty, I knew most families who avoided my family and parents didn't want their children to spend time with me, bringing a sense of isolation. Schools were unable to help me manage my behaviour or help me self-regulate, and although I don't blame school they rejected me and my school exclusion left me even more vulnerable to exploitation.

Had Malcolm approached most 15-year-olds for friendship, they would have avoided him like the plague because he would have represented someone they should fear. However, aged 15, I had experienced care, school exclusion, incredible instability and relationships that created an identity that left me vulnerable to exploitation by him with no relational safety net. In other words, my relationship with Malcolm was a symptom of my life issues and identity, not the cause. He exploited my vulnerability and also used my prison sentence to avoid going to prison himself. You would probably agree if you have read the full story in my earlier book. However I do not believe our relationships started off with exploitation in mind. We found each other through our experience of drug use and marginalisation. He then used his position of power in the relationship to protect himself from harm, at my expense. It may sound like I am defending someone who exploited me in various ways! I am not, just demonstrating the relational experience at the time and how I feel about it now. I am also more interested in preventing it happening to others than I am laying blame at anyone's feet.

Dan Siegal (2009) explains the importance of categorising people in your in-groups and out-groups, exploring 'mind sight' (which is the way we focus attention on the nature of the internal world, the awareness of ourselves, allowing us to focus on the internal world of others). He explains that if one doesn't have the capacity to stay present due to categorising someone as not like you it can shut off the circuits of compassion. We are interconnected by way of relational biology and this needs consideration when tackling youth crime and exploitation. It's a human need to want to feel a sense of belonging, the question is, why do children like I was seek a sense of belonging in unsafe relationships? If such children gravitate towards those with similar life experiences maybe the justice system should capitalise on engaging those who have had similar such experiences. If Siegal's *Interpersonal Neurobiology* (2015) is correct, by demonising the adults young people feel they will become this is likely to cause them to shut down their compassion towards professionals as they will categorise 'us' as not like 'them' and in fact an entity to fear.

I don't believe our current approach is entirely the right one. I believe we should avoid labelling children and demonising adults with complex needs because they are no longer defined as children. We should facilitate relational healing through engaging whole communities, not just individuals. We should share the responsibility for the development of services with those in our vulnerable communities, or villages. Otherwise the young people then gravitate to each other and we further sanction them when they transition as I did through the 'Risk Switch.' This is the consequences of an institutional response to what is effectively a human relational, social and community problem. Child criminal exploitation and crime, particularly youth crime is a cry from some of the most vulnerable children in our society to tell us things are not working for them and others like them. The question at this critical point is, 'Are we going to make it better for the next generation, or are we going to cause more harm for another generation?' Continuing to produce reports about youth custody reform and resettlement which focuses attention on changing behaviour, rather than the underlying causes which are chronic exposure to adversity underpinned by relational and socio-economic poverty.

Children are not isolated tiny humans; they are connected to their relational communities and are dependant on adults to shape their identity as they develop. If we are to now recognise that, for generations, they have been shaped by their relational environments, exploited as a result and then been incarcerated, we must progress further and recognise why so many of these young people gravitate to such relationships. I believe we should accept responsibility and hold ourselves accountable because we have effectively been educating children how to not allow themselves to be shaped by the relational environments provided to them by us as adults. We shouldn't be hailing ourselves as heroes for saving vulnerable people from other vulnerable people because we have the position of power to develop and sustain the narrative when many from these communities simply disagree. Now we recognise children are criminally exploited, we want those very children to view us as the protection from their relational environments. The most effective way to prevent these issues on a societal level is to create a sense of equality and equity and value for those caught-up in the communities in which these issues arise.

- Youth justice interventions need to be more than individualised interventions for children and young people.
- Youth justice needs to be a collective responsibility.
- We must be brave enough to create an alternative narrative where we protect children from any harm, including relational harm, socio-economic poverty and environments linked to criminality which develop identities in various ways including through social interaction and relationships.
- We now know enough about the developing brain and mind to know individualised packages are likely to be ineffective.
- We must push back on the notion of retribution or reparation.
- We know these young people have little to lose which is why punishment has little effect.
- Making them responsible for factors that they have little influence over is likely to be ineffective and ultimately demonises them throughout their childhood developmental stages into adolescence. This seems to me at least to be unreasonable, and contributes towards children being exploited and leaves them seeking safety in the arms of unsafe adults with their own varying levels of unmet need.

- County lines is a slightly more specific element of exploitation by those in positions of power in vulnerable communities and as a result requires a more targeted response.

Is there any evidence that young people feel as I do about how the system operates in terms of relationship building? Let's get the thoughts of three young men that I worked with in various ways as children or young people and explore their feelings on relationships and youth justice. We can ask them how important relationships are to them and what makes good relational justice practitioners. We can examine whether, within a justice context, practitioners can become central relationships in the young people's lives to buffer their experiences of adversity and improve outcomes while still complying with the expectations of the justice system.

Is it models, assessments, interventions and plans, or is it relationships that make that difference to young people in trouble, and if so, what are the key components to relationships in a justice context? Do others believe as I do that lived experience is advantageous with this group of young people in order to have an inclusive system that understands their needs? We have already looked at the literature and my own views based on my subjective reality and knowledge. Now let's listen directly to those with first-hand experience.

CHAPTER 6

Joint Enterprise

Joint enterprise is a legal tag used to encompass groups of people that have been involved together in a crime. It can 'sweep up' those on the fringes as much as the main perpetrators. Some members of that group may not have been directly or actively involved at the centre of a crime but the prosecutor can seek to prove that they did influence or participate in the crime in some way, leaving all defendants to receive the same conviction. In modern times there has been much criticism where those on the periphery of a joint enterprise have received as severe sentences or almost as severe as the main offenders.

However, in a more positive way, or 'flipping the narrative' so to speak, this chapter demonstrates how those with similar life experiences to those that enter the criminal justice system can also influence desistance in others via my version of joint enterprise. I believe we need to define and understand what is meant by *life experience, lived experience* and *living experience* all of which are different. There is some confusion around these concepts and more importantly how services can utilise the perspectives and insights of those that have alternative vantage points of the system or the services we deliver. I will also present my own definition of the *lived experience professional*.

Life experience

As to *life experience*, the definition by Merriam-Webster (2020) works well, i.e. 'experience and knowledge gained through living.' To have similar life experience as any justice service recipient doesn't require someone to have been to prison or have had contact with the justice system, been addicted to drugs or even arrested. It is a shared view of the world due to walking a similar path to the person that you are connecting with. Similar life experience is of course not imperative; however, Tajfel (1979) proposed that groups (e.g. social class, family, football team, etc.) which people belong to are an important source of pride and self-esteem. Groups give us a sense of social identity: a sense of belonging to the social world. As a result, it seems that the contents of this chapter are not controversial or innovative in this regard. This is what we already know about social group membership. Shared life experience creates a natural empathy because 'the mirror properties in our brains enable us to imagine empathetically what is going inside another person' (Siegal 2nd edn, 2015). With shared life experience come similar world views and perspectives and this empathy is therefore from a place of knowing what happens, instantaneously and without effort.

Lived experience

Lived experience is defined in the *Oxford English Dictionary* as

'personal knowledge about the world gained through direct, first-hand involvement in everyday events rather than through representations constructed by other people. It may also refer to knowledge of people gained from direct face-to-face interaction rather than through a technological medium.'

Therefore, if services are seeking to gain the insight of someone with lived experience it would require more than just life experience (above). It would require the insight of someone that has previously experienced the day-to-day journey, e.g. of receiving that service.

Living experience

We often equate lived experience with *living experience* and this is where I think the term is being misunderstood. These individuals are living an experience, as opposed to having *lived* it and moved on, because they are currently caught-up in the issues, e.g. requiring services. This has implications for practice as people living an experience are likely not to have the skills, aptitude or temperament to assist others in a similar circumstance. In addition, agencies will be unlikely to adopt a living experience approach due to safeguarding, confidentiality and risk concerns. Where there are such concerns, opportunities should be limited to those with lived experience, whether they are professionals or volunteers.

Lived experience professionals

I now present my own definition of the *lived experience professional*, because there isn't one readily available, which is:

> 'a person with lived experience of a service or institution that is later employed by that particular service or institution, equal or commensurate to their colleagues.'

These individuals are often like myself, too far down a career or professional development path to speak on behalf of marginalised groups or service recipients. Yes, as we will see, we can be a real asset to services and provide insight of service delivery and be great role models for people currently experiencing similar circumstances.

I believe it is important to have set out these definitions and distinctions so that services are clear what is meant by these terms and subtle differences. It also has to be made clear that not everyone with lived experience would want to share their experiences and so might remain simply a professional. That is a matter of personal preference and should be honoured by their colleagues. I have always been open about my past and experiences and have in fact used them when working with young people. This chapter explores whether or not, on a qualitative basis at least, this was effective in building rapport.

Three interviews

The aim of the interviews that follow is to obtain the views of young adults that have experienced the youth justice system and worked directly with someone with lived experience of the justice system. They have all turned things around and are currently employed, in higher education, or both. They are mature young adults now, so I wanted to obtain their views for this book which I believe is often a missing perspective that provides qualitative, longitudinal insight. I interviewed each person and discussed:

- criminal identity;
- child criminal exploitation; and
- what part relationships and lived experience play within a youth justice context.

I worked with each young person between 2010 to 2019 in varying contexts. Two have experienced incarceration, one was in care and all three were defined as high-risk or persistent young offenders. All three would fall into a hard to reach group while experiencing youth justice. No offences will be discussed in detail for reasons of confidentiality and all have agreed to only their first names being disclosed.

Andrew

Meet Andrew. He was interviewed via Skype from Australia because he now lives there and works on construction sites. I interviewed him during the beginning of the Covid-19 lockdown and he had unfortunately just lost his job due to the quarantine. He was very optimistic about getting a new job so he wasn't fazed by that setback which was great to hear. All professionals in the service that worked with Andrew were pleasantly surprised when I made them aware that he had been accepted and was able to move to Australia. This was because he received a 24 months detention and training order, which is a custodial term for young people, when he was 16.

I first met Andrew when he was released from his sentence. He was subject to a 12 months' licence, six of which would be to work with me on the then named intensive supervision and surveillance programme (ISSP). As he was subject to intensive supervision, this meant he had to spend 25 hours per week with me and my colleagues.

We started the interview by discussing Andrew's offending in general and interventions. Andrew remembers he received a referral order, which is an order for first time young offenders in court, but he can't remember all the details of the offence that resulted in this conviction. I cannot either and as I have already highlighted I will not access any details from the justice system because that would be a misuse of my professional position and it is not really relevant when discussing relationship building. Andrew is no longer subject to any order and, as I worked with him ten years ago, there is no breaking of professional boundaries. This is simply a discussion between two 'consenting adults' for this project.

Andrew remembered the worker he worked with on his referral order. He said he had a good relationship with him, however he only saw him once a week for a short period. He said the intervention was 'pointless' and completely ineffective which he felt was due to the short length of time spent with him rather than any work they did.

I asked Andrew what he felt was the driver for his offending. He initially said that money was. I of course asked him to tell me a little more about his family and background to enable me to dig deeper. I was only two years into my professional career in youth justice at the point of our intervention, so I was being trained in the field. Many conversations were had about his offence, even after he had served 12 months in custody for it. I remember this when I was a young person in the justice system. I would serve a custodial sentence and then spend my licence talking to different professionals about a crime that often happened at least a year earlier. This isn't helpful unless the conversation is led by the young person.

Andrew had served 12 months in custody and children can change so much in this time, so how effective is taking them back to a negative time going to be to build rapport unless they want to discuss the incident? The main reason I remember his offence and the fact that it was acquisitive by nature was because many professional conversations he had with me whilst his qualified officer was present were about it and getting him *to take responsibility*. In fact, we both laughed and recalled a specific conversation whereby his officer stated that he had to take responsibility for the impact on the victim. Andrew always claimed he wasn't at the part of the offence where harm was caused which helped him disassociate somewhat from the victim's experience. They argued about this and, when we left the room together, I recall Andrew saying, 'I can't stand him.' He was stressed as a result of that discussion and that was evident when we left. I knew Andrew well by this point and he didn't become stressed or anxious easily; evidencing that the conversation was detrimental to relationship building, and for what gain I would ask.

Although I was very new to this kind of work and a folk lift truck driver previously, I knew young people in trouble, specifically those that offended, and knew that driving this message home to Andrew would achieve very little, but would damage their relationship. I did try and reflect and be humble and recognise I had a lot to learn. I had to learn how to assess, write reports, manage risk and speak the language the professionals spoke, the jargon. However, I knew how to build relationships with young people involved in crime because I had to do this throughout my four prison sentences and this didn't seem the right approach.

I didn't know it at the time but this was (and is) not a trauma-informed approach, as I also know that being involved in that offence also affected Andrew which is why he responded in this way. He and I discussed this conversation and he just laughed and said, 'I liked him but he was old and stuck in his ways.' He felt it was more about the person's character than his practice which I thought was insightful. It has to be said that this was 2010 and youth justice practice and theory has moved on since then to be focused on strengths, however it remains relevant to understand how and which approaches can damage relationships.

Andrew went on to say that he never had a dad. Although his mother was stable and positive and he feels that she did a good job, he rebelled against his stepfather. As a result, he didn't have a male role model, he looked-up to and he sought relationships out in his local area and the circles he began to move in were criminal. He also said that whilst this was happening and he was in year ten at school, his school changed to a zero-tolerance approach. He couldn't manage his behaviour at this point as he was smoking cannabis which affected it. Due to school exclusion and the message that he wasn't the type of young man that did well there, he built relationships with older peers involved in offending because they too were smoking cannabis and behaved in ways he felt comfortable with. With the need for money increasing and his gravitation to others with offending identities, he said his 'offending became more serious.'

Interestingly, Andrew was clear that his grandad passing also had a real impact due to him viewing his relationship with him as the one constructive male relationship in the absence of his father. However, the pull of the relationships he was developing with his peers were too influential and the 'offending continued to get worse.' Andrew accepted that if he had had a positive father relationship and thus a role model in his life, or had he had a better relationship with his stepfather, things may have been very different. He also stated that although he feels his mum did a very good job, his 'mates within his area growing-up exposed him to lots of offending at a very early age,' which we agreed shaped his criminal identity.

This is important in my view as it demonstrates the link between both Dr Gabor Mate's (2016) explanation of authenticity being sacrificed to fit within social groups. Also, Dr Dan Siegal's interpersonal neurobiology (Siegal, 2nd edn, 2015) around developing a sense of self through experience and relationships. The acceptance of one social group of peers and rejection of education or pro-social groups seemed to help Andrew decide which group he was most likely to be successful in. This could be argued as social marginalisation and may explain that although he had a good relationship with the worker on the referral order, one weekly appointment from Andrew's perspective wasn't sufficient to make any difference to his behaviour or poor choices. This referral order would have required risk-assessment processes but Andrew couldn't remember any such assessment or plan.

Andrew told me that another important factor in his offending was that he was 16 at the time of the offence, one co-accused was 17 and the others were 30, with one being 40. Andrew had never heard of the term *child criminal exploitation*. I explained what it was to him and asked him what he thought. He stated that he didn't think he was exploited and he didn't believe it would apply to young people like him. It wasn't until we explored this further that he agreed it may be the case for what he thought would be other vulnerable young people *but not him*. His next statement didn't surprise me: 'If the group want to commit crime, they need someone to go so why should age matter.' This is a common view of young people within marginalised communities.

Even though Andrew is a mature adult who is no longer in these communities, he understands the language and perspective. So, if these individuals feel like they are together in their challenges we have to find a way of engaging them together to prevent the cycle. Separating or simply disrupting them is compounding their view that they are fighting a system together which is oppressing them, whether subjective or real, and to be effective we need a robust community response.

Andrew and I then went on to discuss his journey through the youth justice system and I asked him to be as open as possible about how he feels now. He started by saying he felt more needed to be done by the system earlier. He felt that he should have received the level of support he received when he was released from custody, but way before he was involved in offending. Andrew told me that he does believe that working with someone with similar *life experience* made a significant difference when leaving custody because of where he was in his offending. However, he did say it wouldn't have been so important earlier on, offering an interesting insight. I then asked him, 'What made our relationship become something that would last to your being 25.' He stated, 'It was because you contacted me even when it had nothing to do with the court order.' This seemed to be significant because it means that it was not just the shared *life experience* or even *lived experience* but the relationship being more than just a professional intervention from his perspective. However, I personally believe being more than professional was in part due to our shared life experience and the lens Andrew thought that I saw him through. *But he didn't say that.*

Andrew described being comfortable in my company and in his words, 'You knew how to read me which was rare for justice professionals,' echoing Siegal's statement that mirror properties in our brains enable us to imagine empathetically what is going on inside another person. Andrew explained that 'Almost every prison officer told me that they expected me to return to prison, especially when I was nearing release.' This is paradoxical to achieving *desistance* from offending as per the literature as desistance, in principle, is moving people on from offending behaviour, not defining them by it. Every time we work with a young person that has extensive experience of the justice system we must acknowledge these experiences.

We may not believe we participate in this behaviour, but not everyone within the system (and they are likely to be within all justice organizations) thinks and behaves in the same way. This is why Risk Relational Paradox is so important. We have to challenge this when we see it taking place or at least listen and be present enough to recognise it and attuned enough to say, sorry.

If we as adults tell young people they aren't able to change, it goes without saying that they are less likely to believe they can. I don't even need to explain that this is not a key component to relationship building. It is something we need to consider when working with young people in trouble because it is their subjective experience and these are our colleagues through the eyes of the young person when they use the word 'system.' This is the responsibility we carry when working with young people and how they view the system as a result of our behaviour. Let's remember, they are still young and are in fact likely to mature and continue to change their behaviour, as do we all through-out our maturation process.

The prison officers Andrew mentioned were unable to view him through the lens via which he deserved to be seen. A young man that was going through a maturity process, even whilst in custody. This is exactly what we as services providers and also as a society expect from young people in his situation. This is in fact implicit bias from the officers to young people in custody. Possibly not so much implicit as explicit and more evidence of the Risk Relational Paradox. These officers clearly didn't believe in change, because their subjective experience is that people come back to prison. If they had lived experience professionals working next to them within the prison this would challenge their bias and offer a different perspective through experience. Maybe, if they had people with lived experience of custody delivering training around how to work with this group and overcome their own bias and show how this is counterproductive, this would improve relationship building and a belief in change. This is an issue that the criminal justice system needs to address because it is in conflict with its own theoretical basis and practice guidelines.

While this was Andrew's experience of offending and the justice system, I asked him what happened to the adults that he offended with. He told me that whilst in custody the adults that we now believe exploited him sent him trainers and money to support him whilst incarcerated. If we view this experience through Andrew's lens, it is easy to understand why he doesn't believe that he was being exploited. Even now, he believes that *they were all in it together* against the system itself that played its part in mistreating Andrew by plac-ing him in custody. Whether he deserved the sentence due to his offending is relevant, but not from the point of how he views the relationships he had with his older peers and those within the criminal justice system. This also highlights a significant difference between sexual and criminal exploitation. Many young people sexually exploited view their exploiters as abusers when they become adults, but this is not the reflections of many we believe to have been criminally exploited. Again, a nuance that cannot be left out of the discussion about how to respond.

Decade after decade we are developing reports of how to reduce the reoffending rate which sits as high as 70 per cent within 12 months post-custody for those under 18 (Prison Reform Turust, 2019). If this is young people's experience of youth custody and professionals within it, this will impact on their own *implicit bias* that those within the system actually care about whether they deter them from offending or not. It is also likely to compound their experience of social rejection and how they feel about the justice system we believe to be the protector. Inadvertently creating a place of safety within the relationships we perceive to be negative and leaving a feeling of resentment or distaste for the very services trying to keep young people in trouble safe. As we have found through the work of Dr Bruce Perry (2016), the brain develops in a use-dependant way. Compassion and empathy are developed by being dealt with in a compassionate and empathetic way. Therefore, if young people continually feel judged through risk-assessment and other punitive relational processes such as Risk Relational Paradox, it seems likely to be an adversarial approach and contribute to the high reoffending rate.

I asked Andrew what in his view made a good youth justice professional and he said they need to be more like 'a friend.' This sat uncomfortably with me as I always saw myself as a friendly professional rather than a friend as such, but I can't pick and choose which parts of the interview I put in this book. I believe this response was due to what I would call 'conditional practice.' I always explain that the system will always have conditions such as plans and objectives, however our relational connection is exclusive of these conditions. I always remember thinking as a service recipient that the two automatically conflate, so if I didn't comply it affected my relationships with the professional and made me want to 'disengage' and avoid contact. This was in part my interpretation of what Murphy (2013) was pointing out about the flaws with contemporary social work claiming to be 'person-centred' when it is more directive and 'State-centred.' However, I believe I mitigated this to some extent by helping the young person to see the two things as being separate. It seemed the main thing for Andrew was that the contact happened when it wasn't required within the context of the justice intervention or national standards. He felt like it was a relationship which was more than just professional. In his words 'Actions speak louder than words.'

The final question from me was, 'Do you think it helps having experience of the justice system when building relationships with professionals?' and his answer was simply, 'Not lived experience of criminality alone, it's about the individual and their character, less about their experience and more about how they treat a young offender.' This is an indication that if we get the key components of relationship building right, we are far more likely to get results of guiding young people away from crime. It is not solely about lived experience, that is just common ground which helped with our relationship, but it was not the only factor according to Andrew. The relationship being the central element, not the intervention, came through loud and clear from Andrew who is now having his time in the sun and I'm sure we all wish him well. He is a great young man and has not allowed his poor decisions or judgements of others to define his future. For that he should be very proud of himself.

Atticus

I invite you to meet Atticus. He is a 27-year-old graduate. There is no getting away from the fact that he and I are quite close. I worked with him in 2009 and 2010 within youth justice and we talk regularly now, a decade later. I have had the blessing of watching him become a man, a father and also qualify in psychology. As with the other two interviewees, I have a communication line with him, which in one way is likely to demonstrate bias towards our relationship and, in another, the point of the effectiveness of relationships in youth justice. I guess different readers will interpret this in different ways.

Atticus has had a lapse and offended on a low level as an adult which unfortunately resulted in a conviction and cost him a potential job opportunity after graduation. It was a one-off incident that doesn't correlate to his offences a decade ago, but convictions have more impact than educational attainment when it comes to application forms, unfortunately. However, this has to be pointed out before we discuss the details of the interview, so we are as honest as possible.

I interviewed Atticus on a warm Saturday morning at a coffee shop. He is currently furloughed from working at a hotel during the Covid-19 lockdown and worried he may not have a job to return to when the hospitality sector returns to its full functions. We started off by discussing his background and how he came to be involved in youth justice and how that felt. He told me,

'I came to the UK from Zimbabwe in Sept 2005 on a family visit to see [my] mum and ended up staying. I found it very difficult because I was a black African boy and I had not seen so many British white people in Zimbabwe, so that was scary. I quickly fell into the wrong crowd in a high crime area and I was trying to fit in and then got involved in street crime.'

I asked Atticus if he felt he could have said no to the group's behaviours. He responded: 'I felt like if I would have said I didn't want to get involved, I would have been pushed out and although I knew it felt wrong, I did it to feel accepted.' A clear example of placing attachment before authenticity to belong in difficult circumstances.

I asked Atticus if he could remember his first contact with youth justice and could he explain how that experience felt. 'I met my first YOT worker in 2009 and he was a black guy like myself but we didn't really have a connection.' I asked why and Atticus stated, 'I felt in some way he was judging me and I was just another black guy that was offending and let him down as a black man.' I found this such a profound thing for Atticus to say when he had previously highlighted not seeing black people was an adversity when he arrived in the UK. I asked him if it was something the practitioner actually said that made him feel that way. Atticus explained,

'No, no, no, it wasn't anything he actually said. The way he would speak you know, we didn't really connect when he interviewed me so, in a way, I ended up just telling him what I thought he wanted to hear.'

This does indicate that we are unlikely to be able to accurately assess the risk young people pose in a risk-management led process if young people like Atticus only tell us what we want to hear, if a human relationship or connection built on trust is not established. This has significant implications because our assessments direct our interventions which affect plans, outcomes and external controls. It is hard to say we are managing the risk if we don't have all the information from the person we are responsible for risk-assessing. This is something I really understand as I was rarely open about risk, or my vulnerabilities, to probation throughout my experience either, because of fear that it would be used against me. This was especially interesting when reading a recent report by HM Inspector of Prisons (2020) that states 'an over-reliance on service user self-disclosure' is one of nine key learnings found in their 'Serious Further Offences Review' new practice guidance. Indicating that if we don't get relationships right it affects our ability to keep the public safe because we are over-reliant on self-disclosure.

'Then you reoffended and came to the ISSP [Intensive Supervision and Surveillance] team which I worked within and I became your key worker. Did you feel having someone with a similar criminal history made a difference to the relational experience in youth justice?' Atticus stated,

> 'Yeah, I really did you know. I felt relaxed and it didn't feel like you were my
> worker, it felt like you were a colleague. I felt like you, Andi, understands it
> so I can relax and speak more freely about things without judgement.'

I had to laugh when he said 'colleague' as I am not sure he would have said that when he was 16. This highlights the importance of framing the narrative with young people. I understand that in ISSP, I had more time to spend with Atticus than his initial case manager which will have also played a role in how he felt about our relationship. Atticus said, 'We would often talk about things that we had in common and not just about me and my behaviour.' His case manager would have been limited in being able to do this with the sheer amount of risk-management processes he was required to do which Atticus didn't even mention and probably didn't understand. This may have contributed to the lack of time to discuss other topics.

I asked Atticus to talk a little about his experience of meeting the victims of his offence in a restorative justice panel.

> 'I remember at the time you saying the victim wanted to meet me and I
> thought, "No way." I spoke to my mum about it and she said do what you

feel is right. After a few more conversations with you, I felt like I would give it a go. I remember speaking to the woman and saying sorry and her explaining the impact of the offence. I knew straightaway that I didn't want to do that to anyone else. The victim at the end of the meeting gave me some flowers, chocolate and a card and that changed me because I didn't offend for a very long time, anyway.'

Atticus has always maintained that this was the most significant factor in his desistance. I also remember him refusing to go through with it originally. It was the relationship that I was able to call on to encourage him to attend in the first place. I say 'encourage' but I can honestly say now it was borderline enforcement through our relationship but he was of course glad he did it in the end.

I asked Atticus to explain what happened after these experiences and what he wants to do in life.

'I wanted to go to university to study and, in 2016, I asked you to write a character reference for me which helped me as I was worried about disclosing my offences. The reference you wrote for me got me accepted into the University of Cumbria in September 2016 and I graduated in July 2019.'

I asked if he felt it was important to be able to come back to the justice system a decade later to ask for that kind of support? Atticus became excited and replied,

'Yes, the reason I felt comfortable coming to you is because we would speak about so much more than offending. We had that connection; no we have that connection never mind had. I just thought surely Andi would be willing to support me with this and you did.'

I am not the only justice professional to have someone come back years after, or to have continued a relationship with a young person in this way. However, the young people are saying the relationship was more important than processes that they are not even mentioning. The question is, are we listening?

The biggest takeaway from the interview with Atticus for me was that even a young black African that felt isolated when arriving in a predominantly white country, felt more of a connection to a white professional that had had contact with the justice system than a black professional who hadn't. Are we going to continue to ignore such an important relational tool while the current justice system is seemingly failing at various levels to achieve desistance for so many persistent young people in trouble? It demonstrates that young people often feel isolated and excluded from society and coming into contact with someone with lived experience feels like a safe relationship without judgement. It is simply a development of relationships they feel they can trust through shared experience, identity and can be explained through neurological development.

I know Atticus' initial case worker and that he was well-respected and also know he is now a manager at a different youth justice team. However, Atticus' interview for me highlights that from a young person in trouble's perspective, or at least from his, it was more about the connection with a practitioner's experiences than the practitioner's knowledge because at that time I knew very little about research, child development or risk-management processes. In 2009, I had just started my degree and had almost no experience of working with this group as a professional. However, due to shared experience, he placed me in his in-group, making him feel unjudged and seemingly gave me access to the relational space that allowed the magic to happen. This allowed my information to be received in a way that helped him along his journey and even encouraged him to meet his victim. This is what he claims was the most significant factor for his future decision to attend university and not offend.

Luke

Let me now introduce you to the wonderful Luke. I interviewed Luke outside Costa Coffee in my car due to not being able to sit in store because it was the day before non-essential stores could re-open after the first Covid-19 lockdown. As Luke is currently studying for a degree in Children and Families, I felt it best to ask questions and let him freestyle his answers as he did not need directing. He is an incredibly insightful young man aged 24 and our relationship or reason we came into each other's lives were slightly different to Andrew and Atticus as

I was not responsible for his order in any way whilst he was in the youth justice system. I will let Luke explain how and why this took place in his own words.

Luke stated that his passage into youth justice started in his early teenage years. He said that he originally got a six months referral order which was at that time the lowest possible court disposal. Luke again stated that he had a good relationship with the worker that managed the order and, when I asked him to expand, he responded, 'We met up around once a week and I did some reparation and we discussed things around my offending and how I could move forward with my life.' At that point Luke was living in a residential home due to being in care and stated he completed his order with very few issues. He said that 'the order coming to an end was a bit of a shame because I felt things were moving in the right direction.' Again, his worker had a good relationship with him and as far as we know has no lived experience of criminal justice. Just reiterating the point that it is not imperative, just helpful.

I asked Luke what kind of conversations he had with his case manager and he stated that they were 'relational conversations about life and how he could use his skills to better his future.' Did he recall if there were any conversations about risk or could he remember any plans or assessments? He said,

'Can't remember any such conversations about risk in any way. I didn't feel he was viewing me through this lens and that is why I would have been happy for the work to continue when it came to an end on a voluntary basis.'

I explained that with a referral order, a risk-assessment had to have been done. That, as a result of this, he would have been assessed as low, medium or high risk which populates the level of intervention. Luke stated, 'I cannot remember this happening.' This is not a surprise as I also know his case manager and believe he would have been navigating the risk-assessment requirements and simultaneously his relationship with Luke. When I became a justice practitioner, it surprised me to know what the professionals that worked with me were doing between my contacts. It shows, in my experience, a disconnect between the functions and the relational experience, between recipient and provider, that we do not discuss.

Luke said that when it comes to *early intervention* in a youth justice context, he feels professionals need to be involved in a child's life for sustained periods of time so the intervention can be built around relationships. He feels that interventions can't be short-term because this isn't how young people build rapport with professionals or with anyone for that matter. Luke feels that as soon as any child is displaying behavioural issues, the justice system should be involved but the emphasis should be to work with them and their peer groups, not just the child as an individual. Luke stated:

'The peer group is everything when you're young, so I believe in early intervention, it just has to be done in a positive way to get the best results for the young people and doing this within the community with peers would be the best way.'

I asked Luke how he felt young people develop criminal identities. Luke felt that:

'Most young people develop criminal identities due to labels. Being excluded from school and being marginalised in the community.'

He also stated that:

'Too much responsibility is placed on young people on the success or failure of their relationships with professionals. Yes, there are differences between young people and how they get involved in crime but there are also a lot of similarities. They need to be addressed and it is not the young person that needs to address them.'

I felt that Luke was reinforcing my view that 'engagement' is not an appropriate word for this group of young people. 'Connection' being a far better description that places emphasis on professionals and services to connect to young people and, if they are not doing so, as many questions should be asked about them as the children they are trying to connect with. Adults and professionals are in a privileged position to be able to say a child 'doesn't engage.' They often fear services and the consequences they see happen to their peers, family members and networks and it is up to us to break down these barriers.

We then moved on to discussing child criminal exploitation and county lines. Asking Luke what he feels about this, he stated that he believed,

> '…these issues have always been present in our communities but that we are now talking about them. We have a label for it and people are aware now so it should be easier to counteract. It is such a broad issue and all young people are at risk of exploitation from one form or another. The best way to tackle exploitation is to surround young people with adults that can protect them.'

Luke seemed to be emphasising relationships and again did not once mention assessment, plans or interventions. Also, I felt it was important to ask him what he viewed as adults that can protect. Luke stated that he felt it was adults that

> 'cared about young people as young people, are attuned to that. It's about sincerity and trust and young people know when they are around someone that cares about them.'

These claims are made in the relationship literature by young people again-and-again. I wonder how good we are at identifying and training professionals that need it and developing this area, if it is so clear and obvious to young people. Tackling this issue would seem to be a logical way to exclude words like 'disengaged' and 'hard to reach' from justice practice.

It is interesting to see that Luke has similar views to myself. I wonder if they are due to similar experiences as service recipients of justice, or sharing so much relational space. This space was as a volunteer for youth justice, not as a service recipient. Luke explains, 'I came back into contact with youth justice as an adult when I met you and became central to the creation of a voice and influence group.' He was a mentor for other young people with care and criminal justice experience and took the role extremely seriously. Luke said, 'I listened to your views of how we can improve the experience for these young people and it made me feel I could contribute in a positive way which I hadn't really considered before.' Again, Luke is explaining that he felt shared experience mattered when it came to having a role model and opening-up his mind to more opportunities for his own future. His mirror neurons connecting with someone that has similar life experiences and views making a positive contribution to helping others which he felt inspiring.

I asked Luke if this experience contributed to him going on to study on a Children and Families course at university. He replied,

> 'Of course it did. I felt a shared optimism spending time with people that felt we could make a positive contribution to service delivery. It also meant I chose to study Children and Families as I want to work in the sector, so volunteering for Leeds Youth Justice Service massively contributed to me taking these steps.'

I hope we all agree that Luke will have a great deal to offer the sector as and when he qualifies, overcomes the barriers and, hopefully, secures himself a position to continue this positive contribution. I have witnessed first-hand how he became a mentor to a young man released from prison that was travelling the merry-go-round of youth custody. It didn't prevent him returning to custody, but the day he was released Luke persuaded him to deliver training to professionals, including the police, around the criminalisation of children in care, which built his confidence and relationships with the police. It seems that utilising the experiences of those with lived experience to work together can have a significant impact on relationship building and building self-worth by using practical examples of change. While simultaneously healing young people in trouble, the process assisted Luke on his own redemption journey.

Analysis

Now we have these lived experiences, lets reflect on Dr Dan Siegal (2017) talking about the mind and how it develops. He explains how relationships are the flow of energy and information and therefore relationships and experience construct the brain's structure and function. Interestingly, Siegal states, 'Experiences can shape not only what energy and information enters the mind, but also how the mind processes that information.' I believe this is relevant because when it comes to marginalised groups, as with myself and all three interviewees above, our experiences led us to decide whose information we validated.

For practitioners working within the justice system, knowledge and information is important, however the delivery of the information through relationships is just as important if the aim is for that information to be transmitted and received effectively. In other words, when our mind has been constructed by experiences, it will dictate how it processes information and where that information comes from. If we do not get the relationships right the information is unlikely to be transmitted effectively. I do not believe this is exclusive to young people in trouble, we all decide about who and where we place merit and who we receive relevant information from.

All three young people interviewed had very different experiences within the justice system, yet all three agreed that information coming from a practitioner that they felt understood their position was better received and more important, even in Atticus' case, than race or ethnicity. I cannot help but ask the question: 'If the young people within youth justice believe this is a key principle of effective practice, why do people with *lived experience* make up such a small minority of professionals within the justice system itself?'

One of the few near certainties in criminal justice is that, for most people, offending behaviour peaks in their teenage years, and then starts to decline. This is the 'age crime curve' (Kazemian, 2007) and, although criminologists disagree on many things, most concur that people grow out of crime through maturation as noted by Andrew Rutherford (2002). Luke said justice professionals need to inspire the young person. I cannot help but believe every young person I work with can change because that belief is entrenched in my DNA. I got through abuse and neglect, care, heroin addiction, exploitation and incarceration to become a justice professional. Most young people I work with do not experience that level of adversity so, in relative terms, they could be my manager in 20 years time.

This so-called curve means most of us grow out of offending by the time we reach adulthood in line with the maturation or construction of the brain as it happens at around 24–25. I am unusual in the sense that I work in youth justice but not unique in the sense that I moved away from offending behaviour. I do not believe I have made so much of an identity change as I have a maturity one, so I am sure we can be more inclusive of others with lived experience. Especially if this is what young people are saying helps in relationship building and that is also reflected in what we know about brain development.

Young people that I have worked with over the years have always claimed to believe that employing people from their own backgrounds with similar identities would help deter them and other young people from offending because they have proved it is possible. Employing people with convictions that have proved they have matured will reduce the risk of them returning to offending as they will have little reason to offend if they are employed. Yet, you will find relatively few ex-offenders that have been incarcerated working within secure settings, probation or youth justice.

Youth Justice Board chair, Keith Fraser (2020) recently took part in a *Guardian* interview with Helen Pidd. He discussed, as a black man, how a white senior police leader didn't take on or embrace his views on community unrest. As a result of their police decisions having the negative impact Fraser predicted, the senior leader apologised later when Fraser was proved right. Fraser stated,

> 'He didn't see it through my eyes and didn't see the potential for what I saw, and that's the value that you get in relation to having different people, whether that's women, diversity or LGBTQ or *whatever*. That difference enables better decision-making and better outcomes. I still don't feel there's enough emphasis on that, there's a bit of lip-service around that.'

When services discuss lived experience or co-production in youth justice, this often transmutes into tokenistic consultation with children currently in the system. Keith Fraser is right, and I would suggest, given the contents of this book, that his 'whatever' should include those with a vantage point of lived experience of youth justice that have turned things around. They could assist those that shape services, undertake the research, or develop tools and interventions to create a more robust and inclusive system in the same way Fraser could see things from his unique perspective.

We are starting to better understand the theoretical and conceptual underpinnings of peer mentoring in the criminal justice system. Webster (2020) invited Dr Gillian Buck to discuss her authoritative review of peer mentoring within it. Dr Buck found that, 'People that have "been there" have credibility and unique knowledge, they are trusted and can be inspirational to others.' Highlighting that they would be a resource to utilise when it comes to making young people vulnerable to exploitation feel there are viable options from peers with similar backgrounds and identities, she also explains that,

> 'Personal experience of going straight offers mentors a credibility that workers don't have. Criminal records can make people feel labelled and excluded, but mentors can try to help people feel valued and included.'

Maybe we can start to think about upskilling those with lived experience within communities to safeguard children alongside authority which would extend the 'social actors' Carlene Firmin discussed in her TEDx Talk around 'Contextual Safeguarding.'

Sean Creaney (2018) in his research also found empirical evidence which indicates peer mentors in youth justice can help young people re-engage with the system. Also, that young people particularly value building empathic and collaborative relationships with professionals who are ex-offenders and have lived experiences of contact with the criminal justice system. There are various reasons this doesn't happen often such as DBS (Disclosure and Barring Service) check issues. However, implicit bias will play its role in the barriers too. Inequality plays its part as academic attainments, gaps in employment history or employment references hold this particular group back, even when they have turned things around. We have placed so much emphasis on theory, process and statistics. This level of understanding the system excludes those that could make a difference but not many in the system say these things matter.

The science and the research we explore in the next chapter indicates that many in the justice system have been swamped with childhood adversity. This therefore requires an inclusive society to provide equity, not just equality of opportunity. This is one industry that could really recognise and utilise their skills while training them to be positive contributors to society. All evidence points towards it being a risk worth taking. After all, it will evidence to everyone that the justice system believes in its own agenda of rehabilitation and retribution. Lived experience alone is not a skill of course. Navigating devastating childhood adversity, the system itself and turning life around is as much a skill as the degree I obtained working in my field. I cannot stress this enough. Even though I know it's an unpopular view, it is clear that young people feel comfortable with others with similar life experience and why wouldn't they? Don't you?

James Docherty from the Violence Reduction Unit in Scotland and I had a discussion about this very subject during the Covid-19 lockdown. Around the importance of the justice system employing others like us as we share a similar background of childhood adversity, addiction and custody. James describes lived experience as the, 'experiential knowing that can get a whole gestalt in one picture.' He believes,

'people with lived experience are the missing link to the problems we are trying to solve in criminal justice. That people seen as the problem need to be a working part of the solution if we are to see any effective change in the system.'

James became a professional over a decade ago after volunteering as I did for services. He obtained employment once his ability to build empathetic relationships and connections with others with similar experience was recognised. He was offered employment which he thrives on today, advocating for change and better outcomes for Scotland's most vulnerable. He recently brought the leading expert Dr Gabor Mate to a conference in Scotland to highlight the social consequences of trauma and childhood adversity. I think it would be fair to say that employing him was a risk worth taking (if ever it was even a risk). He is also someone to be admired and intelligent. He brings far more to the table than his past experiences. He is the very definition of a lived experience professional, if ever I have spoken to one.

A recent Harvard Study undertaken by the Stanford School of Medicine (Humphreys, 2020) uncovered some interesting findings around lived experience in alcohol recovery interventions. After evaluating 35 studies — involving the work of 145 scientists and the outcomes of 10,080 participants — Keith Humphreys, Professor of Psychiatry and Behavioural Sciences, and his fellow investigators determined that Alcoholics Anonymous (AA) was nearly always found to be more effective than psychotherapy in achieving abstinence. Humphreys stated, 'If you want to change your behaviour, find some other people who are trying to make the same change.' Also that although AA is well-known and used by millions around the world, mental health professionals are sometimes sceptical of its effectiveness. I truly believe that justice profes-sionals often have the same level of scepticism about the benefits of including people with lived experience. This may in part be due to the fact that they have worked hard to obtain their education but this does not preclude the effective-ness of unjudgemental social interaction and human connection. There is little to no room for implicit bias from someone that has walked a similar path. As a result, shame gets no energy and doesn't enter the room. This is not exclu-sive to those with lived experience, however it should be the principle aim of every justice practitioner.

Humphreys said,

> 'Psychologists and psychiatrists, trained to provide cognitive behavioural therapy and motivational enhancement therapy to treat patients with alcohol-use disorder, can have a hard time admitting that the lay people who run AA groups do a better job of keeping people on the wagon.'

Early in his career, Humphreys said he dismissed AA thinking, 'How dare these people do things that I have all these degrees to do?' I feel it was brave for Humphreys to admit this, however, in the face of the hard evidence it is hard to argue against the fact that people heal people, not knowledge. We have to find a way of being more inclusive in the justice system of those that experi-ence it and turn things around. They have practical knowledge of the issues and communicate them in ways young people in trouble understand and con-nect with. It really is important to stress, it's just one factor. There are so many others so it does not mean that without life or lived experience you cannot connect using other tools. But dismissing the validation service recipients give to others that have shared being in their position is a mistake the criminal jus-tice system continues to make. We just need to appropriately and safely reduce the barriers that DBS and Criminal Records checks create.

It is worth mentioning that during the Covid-19 crisis, I was redirected to a secure children's home due to service need. I spent 20 weeks working in that secure environment with some of the most complex young people in the country. Also, in what can at times be an emotionally challenging environment as any secure institution can be, I have been able to successfully navigate the experience with no use of any physical intervention and almost no conflict with young people. What did I draw on most? My knowledge or experiences to connect with incarcerated young people? My youth justice degree, or my experience of being in prison and navigating traumatised relationships to ensure I connected with prisoners to prevent violent situations and build relationships with other traumatised individuals? Again, of course, lived experience alone wouldn't be appropriate for so many reasons. I am just making the point that if we can utilise the skills it requires to navigate custody, capitalising on that, creating lived experience professionals, as a result everyone wins.

Neither lived experience nor education alone will create good practitioners, but, whenever we can develop practitioners with both lived experience and education, we should jump at the opportunity because it makes sense. Again, 'a picture is worth a thousand words.' Maybe all aspects of the justice system should recognise this and where possible prove we believe in the redemption script by reducing employment barriers for those with lived experience to become 'lived experienced professionals.'

If I can be trained, with experiences of abuse, care, school exclusion, addiction and prison and make it work, maybe James Docherty is right and lived experience is in fact the missing ingredient to a justice system that would become far more relational and inclusive. Childhood trauma and adversity are experiences that many prisoners like me experienced. Let us explore the literature and examine the relationship this has with offending in the next chapter. Would we reduce offending if we prevented children experiencing trauma?

Postscript

A recent qualitative study conducted by Lenkens et al (2020) exploring the mechanisms of experiential mentoring found that

> 'establishing a strong alliance may be easier for individuals who have had similar experiences to the juveniles they aim to support. An experiential peer may have an advantage over other care providers, since people are more likely to connect with people similar to themselves and deep-level similarities between individuals enhance the quality of the relationship.'

It is fairly reasonable to assume this is an obvious statement. Yet, there is very little motivation for justice services to employ experiential peers due to so little research such as this identifying it as an effective approach to improving desistance. In fact, the perceived risks of employing people with convictions will mean the exact opposite is taking place; inadvertently meaning the criminal justice system is likely to be missing out on the exact individuals that could make it a more relational experience whilst simultaneously making it more effective, by reducing crime and also victims.

In the conclusion of their study, they found that by working together,

'Experiential Peers may pave the way for clients' receptiveness to more specialized help. Respectful and appreciative collaboration may also lead to an overall more recovery-oriented perspective within the organization, in which the client perspective becomes more important. Collaboration may thus be able to improve the care for adolescents and young adults with criminal behaviour. These youths often come from disadvantaged backgrounds in which recognition and appreciation were lacking. Regaining trust in one person that they can relate to, even if it is minimal, can be a first step away from criminal behaviour and towards desistance' (Ibid).

CHAPTER 7

Youth Crime and Trauma

Before we explore the links between youth crime and trauma, I thought it best to examine the concept of trauma itself. The one thing we know for sure is that trauma is not just one thing. It is more how people experience an event or events that makes something traumatic. This makes it almost impossible to define and as I am not a psychiatrist, psychologist, therapist or clinician I will not attempt to. Reading Dr Bessel Van Der Kolk's work *The Body Keeps the Score* (2015) was my first real in-depth insight into trauma and how it impacts on individuals. Van Der Kolk states that:

> 'We have learned that trauma is not just an event that took place sometime in the past; it is also the imprint left by that experience on mind, brain, and body. This imprint has ongoing consequences for how the human organism manages to survive in the present. Trauma results in a fundamental reorganization of the way mind and brain manage perceptions. It changes not only how we think and what we think about, but also our very capacity to think.' (Ibid)

This implies that experiencing trauma impacts the very capacity to think changed by the experience. So, what about children experiencing trauma?

It is very important to recognise Van Der Kolk's statement when thinking about trauma and youth crime; especially how to intervene to improve or modify a young person's perception of the relational world they operate in. Trauma, so far as I understood it before reading *The Body Keeps the Score* was an event or incident that had lasting consequences for the individual that experienced it.

My childhood consisted of abuse, neglect, violence, exploitation, instability and uncertainty. Although there were several events that felt traumatising that I remember, I wouldn't have understood these or described them as trauma.

Interesting that throughout my journey through the criminal justice system, including prison, professionals tried to change or improve my thinking but had very few conversations about how my childhood shaped that thinking. In fact, I learnt to stop discussing my childhood as I was often told this isn't an excuse to shut a conversation down. How difficult is it to improve a young person's capacity to think and wouldn't it be easier to focus resources on preventing the events that impair the capacity to think in the first place? Would this be an effective approach to preventing youth crime? Let's explore these questions in more detail.

The ACE studies

We have long since had a wealth of knowledge of childhood development and how, during early developmental stages, abuse or neglect and disrupted attachment relationships with primary carers negatively impact children's health and the child's life course. We have more recently made significant progress in understanding how this can cause biological problems for humans as they develop into adolescence and beyond. The findings of the 'Adverse Childhood Experiences (ACE) Study' (Felitti et al, 1998) were groundbreaking in the sense that the study found a dose response relationship between the level of adversity experienced as a child and lifelong health issues such as hepatitis, depression, high blood pressure and lung cancer among others ('dose' is a way of describing response to a stimulus or stressor). The research was based on an epidemiological study which explored the incidence, distribution and possible control of diseases and other factors relating to health.

In this study 'adversity' was defined as physical, emotional or sexual abuse, physical or emotional neglect, parental mental health, substance misuse, parental incarceration, parental separation or domestic violence. These adversities are almost always experienced through relational connections a child has within the context of family, environment or community. They are experiences that disproportionately affect those families that are faced with systemic and structural inequality, intergenerational trauma and socio-economic hardship. These experiences are intrinsically linked from parent to child biologically and environmentally and more often than not manifest into relational poverty and marginalisation. In the words of Van Der Kolk (2015) himself,

> 'the ACE study has shown that child abuse and neglect are the single most preventable cause of mental illness, the single most common cause of drug and alcohol abuse, and a significant contributor to leading causes of death such as diabetes, heart disease, cancer, stroke, and suicide.'

This indicates that if we could prevent child abuse we would improve health outcomes across the board whilst saving spending on the economy such as the NHS, social care and justice services.

Within the original US ACEs study, they examined 17,000 participants, making it the largest study on childhood neglect and abuse. The participants were not necessarily exposed to the typical risk factors that lead young people into crime; in fact, the participants were not specifically selected from areas of deprivation at all. The participants were insured for health costs, educated and employed, which is important to highlight. They were asked ten questions which covered all the aforementioned adversities during their childhood years. The results of the study have manifested themselves into movements all over the world to recognise the biological health impact that these adversities can cause throughout the life course.

It was hoped by many that western societies would finally evolve from shaming marginalised groups such as parents of children in care, drug addicts, prisoners and the homeless to looking at them through an empathetic lens and trying to understand where the behaviours come from. Unfortunately, these movements have been limited in achieving that aim, although it is significant that some institutions have shifted their focus from asking not 'What have you done?' to rather 'What happened to you?' Although this is in some way progress, the focus as a result of such findings should always be preventing the harm, as opposed to responding to it.

The English ACE study

The first thing to recognise is that the English study undertaken by Bellis et al (2014) found that almost half (46 per cent) of the adult population in England had at least one ACE, while eight per cent had four or more. As in the USA, there was a dose relationship between the number of ACEs and poor health outcomes. Interestingly, in the context of youth justice, individuals with four or more ACEs were three times more likely to smoke, seven times more likely to have been involved in violence in the past year and eleven times more likely to have used heroin or crack cocaine or been in prison. Does this mean if you are raised in poverty, you are more likely to make poor life choices? Have we created services that are joined-up in a coherent way that ensures we can travel along an intergenerational cycle with humans as they develop and grow from children into adults; or do we fragment the life journey into episodes such as childrens' and adult services making humans fit into services instead of the other way around?

Toxic stress and exposure to other adversities

The science behind the research is that toxic stress (Harvard University, 2020), not positive or tolerable but profound stress, which leads to the body excessively producing cortisol or adrenaline, causes biological damage to a developing child. The National Scientific Council on the Developing Child (Shonkoff et al, 2007) stated, 'The essential feature of toxic stress is the absence of consistent, supportive relationships to help the child cope.' This indicates that although a number of ACE studies highlight that a large proportion of countries like the US and UK experience adversity, as children these factors are most damaging when they happen in the absence of attachments to consistent, supportive relationships.

Parental separation is defined as an adversity within Felitti's study. However, if both parents understand the stress their break-up can cause for their child and do everything they can to reduce the stress levels it is extremely different to how it was with myself who has never seen his father, and whose mother was only 16 when she conceived him. This is an example of how ACE questions are not an exact science. They do not incorporate the complexities of the human life experience or how they can be buffered through supportive relationships or emotionally available, co-regulated adults.

An experience of high doses of adversity during childhood in the absence of supportive adults doesn't just affect the developing brain structure and function, it negatively impacts on the developing immune system and even how our DNA is read and transcribed. Dr Nadine Burke Harris (2015) discusses this in her TED Talk (Harris, 2015) 'How Childhood Trauma Affects Health Across a Lifetime.' This explains the recent shift in trauma-informed questions asked by professionals as complex trauma isn't necessarily what happens to you, it's what happens inside you. The impact of that trauma needs buffering through relationships and nurture. If the youth justice system wants to place relationships at the heart of practice and deliver on its 'Child First, Offender Second' principle, we need to develop key components of effective relationship building and have a discussion about risk-management being its primary function and how institutional risk-management processes impact on these relationships.

Robert W Block, the past president of the American Academy of Paediatrics stated that,

> 'Children's exposure to Adverse Childhood Experiences is the greatest unaddressed public health threat to our time.'

Although not all children who experience high levels of ACEs will go on to commit crime, most young people in custody as we will explore have experienced a chronic and persistent dosage of ACEs or grown-up in a stressful environment which negatively impacted their development. Just like myself, these children are unlikely to view themselves as victims of relational harm in adolescence. Not at a stage where they have built resilience to help them manage their relational environments. Opening-up about this is likely to feel as if it will render them vulnerable at a cost of their peer relationships. It would seem logical to me that all interventions should navigate this complexity in a sensitive way.

The impact of ACEs

Ford et al (2019) discovered in a Welsh adult male prison population that prisoners with four or more ACEs were four times more likely to have ever served a sentence in a young offender institution (YOI) than those with no ACEs. They also found 46 per cent of the adult prison population had spent time in one. Therefore, the more adversities experienced in a young prisoner's life, the earlier they are likely to come into contact with the justice system which often results in longer periods of offending. So it is argued by Ford et al that 'the strong relationship found between ACEs and youth, prolific and violent crime indicate prevention of ACEs could provide a significant opportunity to reduce crime.' This was exactly the same argument made by Case and Haines (2015) with their 'Child First, Offender Second' approach, accepted by the Youth Justice Board as a key principle to guide the youth justice system. However, prevention in a youth justice context is often pre-arrest. We have already explored identity formation, indicating that early intervention needs to take place in the early stages of development, not only when behaviour is defined as criminal. If offending behaviour is prolific or serious, it's an indication that previous opportunities have been missed.

There seems to be a philosophical and social discussion about ACEs and how services should respond. Does the research pathologise parents who are simply exposed to systemic and structural inequalities which renders them vulnerable in their own right? Is it a risk-focused, deficit model that doesn't consider the resilience of children to manage stress and adversity? My high exposure to a chronic dosage of ACEs happened within my family home and relationships. However, mum was in care and fell pregnant with me aged just 16 after experiencing abuse and neglect which clearly traumatised her. When it comes to intergenerational trauma passing from parent to child, like from mum to me, we need to be careful not to forget the community context in which this happens and the role relationships and community play. Research around ACEs proves that inequality and inequity disproportionately impact on our vulnerable families. We must however make sure we don't blame parents alone, as my mother needed a village to help her raise me due to capacity issues resulting from her abuse. The research, as far as I am concerned, simply tells us what I already knew, which is that too much adversity for children causes harm and that society is failing our vulnerable families. If we prevent ACEs, we will improve the life outcomes of every child. It's not a model, it's a wake-up call to society.

Parental incarceration and exposure to criminality

Although one of the questions in the ACE study is about parental incarceration, I have found little research undertaken about experiences of exposure to criminality during developmental stages of childhood and how this can shape an identity. This is what took me into exploring the work of Siegal (2015) and Perry (2016). As criminality is a behaviour and we have found that behaviour of adults plays a significant role in the development of any child's identity, this lack of attention seems like a shortcoming within youth justice research. Parental incarceration is recognised as an adversity, but what if criminality is prevalent but the parents have not been incarcerated? A study undertaken with adult offenders found after

> 'a review of the literature and current findings, criminal behaviour can be added to the host of negative outcomes associated with scores on the ACE Questionnaire. Childhood adversity is associated with adult criminality. We suggest that to decrease criminal recidivism, treatment interventions must focus on the effects of early life experiences.' (Reavis et al, 2013)

However, this doesn't indicate which of the ACEs is most linked to adult offending, just that criminality is a negative outcome of ACEs.

Is it traumatic for children to witness the consequences of criminality such as police presence, exposure to criminal networks and carers in conflict with authority? Are we incarcerating those young people with most exposure to what I describe as relational criminality? Do we then view them through a lens of lacking resilience when they are in fact shaping their behaviour and suppressing their authenticity to survive criminal and volatile environments?

In his video 'How Relationships Shape Us,' Siegal (2017) when talking about attachment, states, 'The way a parent interacts with their baby, will determine that baby's capacity for self-awareness and awareness of others. It's an inborn potential that needs experience to develop well.' And if trauma impairs that development as stated by Van Der Kolk, it is likely that this is going to impact on social interactions and gravitation to familiar relationships due to shared experience. Therefore, the exposure to criminality itself may not be a traumatic experience, but the response of society being marginalisation and incarceration can cause isolation, adversity and trauma.

On a personal level, this is exactly how it felt sitting in a prison cell after being criminally exploited aged 17. I couldn't understand what had happened along the way due in part to a lack of capacity and of safe, containing adult relationships that could have helped me reflect on my childhood and make sense of my own identity and exposure to harm. This cannot be done through a short intervention and is certainly made harder during incarceration. It is an incredibly lonely place to be at adolescence during a critical phase in brain development. I was being punished for my actions but not supported and educated to understand the factors that most influenced them. When young people transition through what I call a 'Risk Switch' (see later in this chapter), we must embed their childhood experiences in our minds as professionals to better understand and empathise with their behaviour as adults. If ACEs tell us anything, it is that the childhood experience lives with the individual in both mind and body, so why not behaviour?

Potentially harmful youth justice processes

Trauma is often intergenerational and doesn't happen in a vacuum. Vulnerable children become adults, but it doesn't mean the experiences of that child are no longer relevant to their behaviour. This makes me think of a quote of a young man in care with a care experienced mother I met at a group event I organized who said, 'You are telling me to change, but you're not telling me how.' This demonstrates motivation but also an inability or incapacity to embrace the support we are providing. He wasn't capable at the time of influencing many aspects of his relational environment and we were limited in our capacity to influence his capacity. The default position within our society when this happens is to fall on the last resort of punishment or prison. This can compound marginalisation and creates a fantasy that punishment fixes trauma by using words like rehabilitation. This word in my view is often used out of context: rehabilitation in the English dictionary means the action of restoring someone or something to its former position. However, these individuals have never been in a position we can claim we are trying to get them back to. Their predisposition is often handed to them from birth intergenerationally, as was mine.

The impact on children entrenched in traumatising and criminal relationships of subsequent relational poverty and social exclusion is underestimated by society. All three young men I interviewed for this book (*Chapter 6*) felt they had a good relationships with their justice practitioner in the beginning, but there wasn't enough contact to build a truly authentic relationship. I had various professional relationships growing-up but none stable or consistent enough to mitigate the developmental harm I experienced during childhood which led to toxic stress. The vast amount of young people in youth justice have already experienced school exclusion or even contact with children's support services, in varying capacities. This demonstrates to me some level of institutional response from 'the village,' as other services have not been able to halt their negative life trajectory. Instead of receiving consistent relationship-based support from services to tackle adverse environments that cause harm, they seemingly pass through services with various professionals with their own assessment and intervention models. What these children and their families often require from services are supportive relationships, not institutions, referrals and processes but continuous, consistent supportive care.

If a traumatised child experiences relational inequality and exclusion from institutions such as school and youth clubs, they will always be able to rely on their family's networks for attachment and human connection. The safest place for a dysregulated child with behavioural problems to feel unjudged and accepted is with other dysregulated peers. I know this because I experienced the sense of rejection myself and it is in fact part of the 'Risk Relational Paradox.' The child of course perceives rejection as a risk and as a result learns to avoid being rejected. I perceived services as a risk to myself and my networks and this left me at risk of exploitation. It may seem a challenge, but we have to find a way for youth justice services and others to become an embedded, trusted part of marginalised communities, to challenge from within as a force created to protect children in the eyes of everyone, not just us as 'authority.' We often talk about the interface between organizations and services; however, we need a discussion about this interface between services and communities, not just working with individuals but how we engage whole communities in an interconnected way.

This may also explain why, over the past decade, I have continually rec-ognised the children's surnames when they enter the justice system. I was in prison with many of their fathers. It would seem it is social programming and relationships, not just trauma, social rejection or adversity which plays a role in the development of a criminal identity. The intersectionality and nature of such factors significantly increases the likelihood of a child developing a crimi-nal identity. It is not solely a biological response to developmental trauma but also an intrinsic self-perception developed through their relationships, more often than not familial.

We all need a sense of belonging and we have shaped society in a way that leaves the marginalised dependant on the marginalised. We then provide ser-vices that educate them, effectively blaming them for their own disadvantage or believing that they lack resilience. We have convinced ourselves that people are solely responsible for their decisions which is only in part true because we as humans are social creatures and need others to survive and live. Decisions are led by identity which is predominantly shaped by relationships, often as Dr Dan Siegal states in his talk 'How Relationships Shape Us,' 'before we have a conscious mind.'

There are of course no determinant factor(s) for youth crime, but indicators which significantly increase likelihood just in the same way ACEs are not deter-ministic on an individual level. Exposure to criminality through attachment relationships, which I call relational criminality, combined with the conse-quences of trauma or adversity does go some way to identify which children are most at risk. It is a cycle of abuse and explains my truth that most of those I met along my journey through the prison system were *good people*.

If many prisoners were being honest, just like me, they often don't fully-understand their own behaviour and the root causes which inevitably leaves them with a sense of shame and the self-identity of being a *bad person* that needs to be imprisoned to protect others from them. I simply refused to sub-scribe to this. ACEs at least offer me some insight and context into my own poor choices. I could not articulate to professionals what was going on inside of me and, when I tried, I was often described as 'challenging,' or it was said that I wasn't taking responsibility. Just because someone is not able to tell you a message in a way you understand doesn't mean we shouldn't listen. This is what I describe as attunement, which all justice professionals need.

Prison is not in my view the best indicator of morality as many may believe for most that sit within it. For a large number, including those that experienced separation and loss as children, it is more an indicator of those that are using problematic behaviours such as addiction or crime to deal with childhood complex trauma and adversity. Many have sought addictions in various ways to access hormones such as serotonin, dopamine and endorphins to promote feelings such as happiness, positivity and even love, due to the pain, isolation and sadness that many have experienced in their early years. We as services have been limited in our ability to provide alternative ways of healing or replacing their pain with love, care and nurture. It says just as much about how we have developed services and society as a whole as it does about the individuals, in my view. Again, especially those adults in custody that have come into contact with services early in their childhoods. It is not about shifting responsibility as much as it about understanding the context of the behaviour we are trying to change and how risk plays a role in communities many prisoners come from.

Whilst I served my four prison terms from the ages of 17 to 23, I witnessed first-hand prisoners in various offending behaviour or thinking skills programmes try and articulate ACEs in their own way to professionals and how they impacted on their choices and relationships. Of course, when they were challenged on their views, their stress response system was activated and they struggled to maintain attention or focus on the conversation. This doesn't lend its hand to articulating what we know about the biological response to toxic stress, even if they knew that.

The justice professionals then record that we are abusive and we don't take responsibility for our crimes, and increase risk levels which leads to further sanctions or consequences and, as a result, creates further distrust of justice professionals. We need an in-depth conversation about ACEs, complex trauma and the criminal justice system which involves those that have recovered from these experiences. This would likely improve how these interventions are delivered and develop trust in the 'system' and make it more effective and responsive to the needs of those within it.

ACEs and social inequality

The ACEs and Social Inequality Window below demonstrates my view of the interaction or interface between Relational Wealth, which is the emotional and attuned availability of carers or adults for children as they develop, and Economic Stability. If a child is provided with both of these things they are of course still likely to face some level of adversity, as found in the English ACE study (Bellis et al, 2014). However, children developing in the absence of both are far more likely to face a larger dosage of ACEs. As we now know, the larger the dose of ACEs, the higher the likelihood of poor health and social outcomes due to toxic stress. This is also due to the lack of access to supportive nurturing adults to mitigate or buffer the experience (Shonkoff, 2007). That is how structural inequality, intersectionality and intergenerational trauma come into play. The very children that have the least regulation to tackle adversity are the same children that experience most adversity, which leads to developmental trauma, making the stress they experience toxic. Add the attachments for the child or adolescent being adults involved in criminality throughout development and we start to understand it is often more than simply poor choices when it comes to serious and in particular prolific youth crime.

The ACEs and Social Inequality Window can be used to develop empathy and to understand that growing-up in economic hardship, or in deprived areas, alone does not make it okay to have the belief that you didn't make poor life choices, so why do others. We do not develop regulation or the capacity for attachment alone as developing children. We need attachments to nurturing, supportive adult relationships to develop our innate potential of attachment and regulation. A child could live in economic stability and miss out on emotionally attuned adults and be abused in various ways. A child can also live in poverty and have attuned, nurturing adults that develop regulation and secure attachment. I am going to demonstrate that the vast number of children we have always incarcerated have lacked both economic stability and supportive attachments. They are also faced with the most difficult life choices, and often, as a result, get them wrong like I did.

Developmental trauma which is of course my new understanding of trauma refers to a type of stressful event that occurs repeatedly and cumulatively, usually over a period of time, and within specific relationships and contexts. Childhood abuse (sexual, emotional, and physical) and neglect (physical and emotional) constitute typical forms of chronic traumatisation (Courtois, 2004). Not rarely, families with dysfunctionalities such as, for instance, affect dysregulation among family members, may also be developmentally traumatising for their offspring (Ozturk and Sar, 2005), but many like me are unlikely to understand this as traumatic. Many young people we incarcerate believe they have lived 'normal childhoods' due to not understanding their experiences as traumatic. It is only when you delve into their background that you understand these experiences are traumatising which often provides context to behaviour.

ACEs AND SOCIAL INEQUALITY WINDOW

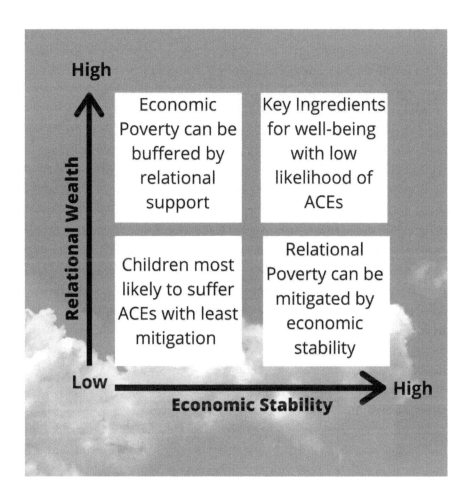

This is often how trauma becomes intergenerational. If you believe what happened to you didn't cause any harm and you are 'okay,' it is likely that subconsciously the behaviour will be passed to offspring relationally and environmentally, not just biologically. The image of the child we hold in our mind as parents is rooted within our own experience of childhood and of being parented. This is something I am forever grappling with as a parent to a four-year-old after spending my first two decades entangled in intergenerational trauma, social rejection, exploitation, addiction and prison.

I believe I am a good father, but I am not blinded by the delusion that my life experiences haven't shaped me. I am just blessed to have developed reflection as an adult and been lucky enough to access supportive relationships that have helped me reshape my own behaviour over recent years and for that I feel blessed. It also comes with the burden of shame for others not so blessed. My wife and daughter simply make me a better person; however, my childhood does play a role in my household in various ways. None more so than my relationships with family and siblings having children removed or with toxic addictions.

While I was subject to the criminal justice system as a young person in trouble, I tried to articulate the effects I have described in this book. That I was angry and impulsive as far back as I could remember. Years before the age of ten (the age of criminal responsibility), again indicating prevention in identity development is not the same as preventing arrest or conviction. I was taking drugs heavily aged 12, excluded from school aged 15 and addicted to Class A drugs while my peers sat their exams. This meant I was rejected by people around me when relationships were what I needed to mitigate against the relational adversity and increased stress levels. Ironically, it was the relationships I experienced as I developed that were simultaneously the root cause of adversity, leaving me vulnerable to criminal exploitation. If we as a society don't hold our hands out to catch a dysregulated or challenging child, dysregulated or disaffected older peers who have progressed through the Risk Switch will be there instead. What message does that child receive when we judge or punish that older peer because he or she may also have poor outcomes due to trauma or chronic exposure to ACEs?

Becoming a professional and finding out about ACEs, toxic stress and complex trauma helped me to better understand the impact on my own childhood and the link with my poor choice of relationships. This isn't about shifting responsibility, but understanding the relational context to behaviour and actions. The question is, why as a society have we become so hung up on making young people responsible for youth crime, and not making society aware of the why? Shame, guilt, inequality and disempowerment are often the factors that contribute most to young people entering the justice system in the first place. The aim of that system therefore could be to address any shame through building relational networks for the young person. Instead it involves a very low criminal age of responsibility, handcuffs, prison, courts, punishment and educating the child to not be socially marginalised through individual educational interventions.

It surprises me then why we wonder what sits behind the high reoffending rates for those young people we incarcerate. They are so high for the most prolific and serious risk young people because their relational networks are not conducive to change; the incarceration experience reinforces their identity as outsiders and, upon release from custody, their opportunities of inclusion become even fewer and further between. As a society, we see them through a deviance lens, often driven by media and public perception of criminals, not recognising their maturity or behaviour as a symptom of various problems, often outside of their control. We then create a narrative that there is something wrong with the them, not that they are adapting to traumatic environments that we as adults constructed for them to develop in. However, in truth, it is more often than not their relationships or environment that need the intervention. 'When a flower doesn't bloom, you fix the environment in which it grows, not the flower' in the words of Alexander Den Heijer.

Jacobson et al (2010) found that a youth justice system that puts more emphasis on addressing welfare needs instead of punitive measures is likely to achieve better results. Their argument was grounded in the same principle as Ford (2019). That if the justice system prevents exposure to the risk factors or ACEs that develop into offending, it is likely to reduce the children coming into contact with the justice system. This seems like a completely reasonable position to take up and one I agree with in terms of prevention when we explore the literature and examine the types of children that end up in youth custody. However, we must also focus on changing criminal identities to ensure justice measures are targeted in the right area post-offending; not just addressing trauma or adversity.

The intergenerational argument does indicate that the prison system needs to produce good parents, not just good citizens, if we are to challenge the cycle of abuse and transition of identity which, as we have already explored, develops through relationships. Education around the content of this book is essential in prisons. Ex-prisoners such as myself and others doing (what I believe to be) immense work in the UK make great facilitators for leading that change of identity. Yet again, a picture paints a thousand words.

Bessel Van Der Kolk (2005) explains that childhood traumas are very common and have a profound impact on many different areas of functioning. Explaining that if

'a child grows up with an alcoholic parent, that child is very likely to have a multi-faceted symptomatic response that is likely to include depression, various medical illnesses as well as a variety of impulse and self-destructive behaviours.'

This is good to know if you have had a childhood like mine and made poor relational choices because most adults that brought me up had mental health and substance misuse problems due to their childhood trauma. Some have died very early and others are in prison or homeless but almost all have had poor outcomes. This exposure to traumatised adults had a significant impact on my behaviour but received very little work or attention during my journey through the justice system. Not a single professional ever said anything of the sort in my journey to recovery. This seems to be selective education, as I did Business Studies and Sports courses and was taught about rights and responsibility. That was a sole focus on how my behaviour impacted on others. I heard very little about the impact of the behaviour of others on my development. There may be various reason for this, such as professionals not wanting to give young people an excuse for their behaviour or not wanting to 'open-up a can of worms,' which I hear a lot. However, if young people don't understand the context themselves, how would they start to change it?

As already stated, I am not drawing a causal link between childhood trauma, toxic stress and offending. There is no one single causal factor leading to offending or criminality. Even with a further generation of research, we will never find a causal link to youth crime in my view because there are simply too many variables. There are too many factors in a life journey leading towards a criminal act and too many types of crime to ever draw a definitive conclusion. Identity is the most significant factor for youth crime in my experience which is reflected in desistance theory. It is often interconnected with racism, substance misuse, school exclusion, relational criminality, exploitation and childhood trauma.

Children want to feel a sense of belonging to others which is a basic human need because we are social and this is how we construct our sense of self. When others are involved in serious or prolific crime, it is often because they feel good at crime and get recognised for the skills they bring to the criminal table. If they have been marginalised and excluded for not fitting the social expectations of pro-social groups (often due to not being able to manage their emotions due to trauma and adults and peers accepting them for their criminal identity and skills) it makes complete sense that as children, at least, they will gravitate to where they feel accepted, for safety reasons. This is often a reason many of this group say they like to work with professionals with lived experience. It is not what the professionals know, it is who they perceive them to be that creates a safe space for them.

Trauma or adversity not being the sole driver or causal factor for youth crime doesn't let us as a society off the hook by the way. One thing we know for certain is that developmental trauma often causes dysregulation in child-hood. Emotional dysregulation may be thought of as the inability to manage the intensity and duration of negative emotions in social contexts. We cannot ignore that many of the young people we incarcerate experience trauma and adversity amongst many other factors. These children don't lack resilience, rather the resilience they have developed to tackle their environments simply does not fit in with social norms when they reach adolescence.

Trauma may not be a causal factor on an individual level; however, it under-pins many social issues that impact on life outcomes and relational integration. Therefore, on a societal level, a focus and a reduction of the impact of intergen-erational trauma and ACEs will inevitably lead to a reduction of youth crime. Not every young person I was incarcerated with was traumatised, but it was obvious most had experienced traumatic events and displayed dysregulation. I wonder what they would have done had I said, 'Come on guys, we're just a little dysregulated right now.' On second thoughts, maybe not.

Lord Laming (2016) in his exploration of the link between care and crime found that 94 per cent of children in care do not enter the youth justice system while they are in care. It is fair to assume that almost every one of these children would have experienced a high dosage of ACEs or complex trauma in their childhood and yet they haven't come into contact with the youth justice system as children. This is evidence that not all children who experience trauma or are even separated from their birth family come into contact with the justice system. In fact, most do not. It is why I believe focusing on trauma or adversity within the criminal justice system post-offending and not identity would fall short of supporting desistance or reducing reoffending.

There are of course two conversations to be had. One concerning how to prevent youth crime of which a reduction of ACEs and trauma would significantly impact as found by Ford (2019) and Jacobson et al (2010). The other how to support desistance for those that have entered the justice system and developed a criminal identity. Both are important in equal measure. Andrew in *Chapter 6* articulated this well in his interview. That lived experience only matters when a young person has developed a criminal identity, not before.

Furthermore, although in Laming's (2016) independent report it states that 25 per cent of the adult prison population have been in care, this doesn't tell us much about these individuals' childhoods, other than exposure to some level of unfortunate family circumstance and separation. However, thinking about those young people in care I have worked with who enter custody, many reflect the findings of HM Prisons and Probation Service's report on 'Care Leavers' (2019), that entry into care in adolescence and maltreatment has a stronger influence on offending than maltreatment alone. In fact, from my experience at least, almost all young people that have care experience who become incarcerated enter care late. They enter for short periods, have criminality present within the family network and continue to have contact with their families throughout their care experience, often not in agreement with children's social work services.

The reason I highlight this is because it is suggestive of the fact that although traumatic experience correlates with those we incarcerate, the most common correlating factor is a criminal identity constructed by exposure to adults and peers involved in offending throughout their development. Children develop the behaviours through contact with carers, wider family members or peers within a community context. This may also explain the commonalities between those in youth custody that have, and those that have not, experienced care and family separation, as highlighted by the Youth Justice Board (2015).

Separation at adolescence from carers simply compounds negative childhood experiences. This at least challenges the idea therefore that the behaviours are simply a matter of personal choices of the young people. It also shines a light on the challenges the care system has with the behaviour of those that enter care late which I have witnessed over the years. This should of course be reflected in the age of criminal responsibility which is currently ten-years-old in England and Wales and not internationally accepted by the United Nations Convention on the Rights of the Child (Youth Justice Legal Centre, 2016).

Taking all this into account, I therefore draw the conclusion that the development of a criminal identity through interpersonal relationships has a far stronger correlation to offending in young people than either trauma itself or the care experience. Of course, these factors are likely to affect the child's life course and development. However, relational criminality seems to have more impact on the development of a criminal identity which leads to a gravitation towards criminal relationships. The Youth Justice Board (2015) in their response to Laming did state that there was a crossover of risk factors between children who enter youth justice and those who enter the care system. The shared ground is often poverty, abuse, neglect and inequality, not always criminality within relationships pre-care or post-care. It is possible for parents to not be able to meet their children's needs, e.g. but not live in high crime areas or be involved in crime themselves. It is possible that they may have unmet needs themselves which impacts on their capacity to parent appropriately, but that has little to do with criminality or anti-social behaviour.

If only six per cent of children in care enter the youth justice system, but 25 per cent of those in adult prisons have been in care (Laming, 2016) what does that tell us? The prison population of care experienced people is likely made up of those who enter care late in adolescence, or like me for a short period of time. It seems very likely that most have gravitated towards criminal relationships due to those relationships being familiar. Maybe, the care system is a little more successful when it comes to supporting identity change than it gets credit for?

I am certainly not advocating more children go into care, or even that the care system doesn't have shortcomings for those care leavers who disproportionately end up homeless or with addictions. Recent reports are highlighting the damage privatising children's homes is having on accessibility or unregulated accommodation has on care leavers (Children's Commissioner, 2020). I am simply highlighting that if relationships are the key to reshaping identity, it seems to be quite successful in ensuring children are at least for the period of time whilst in care avoiding the youth justice system, even though there is a crossover of risk factors. I would imagine this may be an unpopular position to take up and not one I had when I started out working with care experienced people in the justice system. However, I am more interested in reducing recidivism than falling into my own subconscious bias in the face of all the evidence about identity formation.

I of course recognise that children in residential homes have historically been criminalised far too early (Department of Education, 2018). However, in my professional and personal experience, which I think together are fairly extensive now, these types of offences do not automatically develop into later prison sentences. If a child or young person enters care at the age of ten-years-old and eventually enters a residential home, it would be a lack of understanding trauma, criminal behaviour and desistance to simply lay blame at the hands of residential staff or social care for their behaviour. Not that I am making a direct comparison by any means, however prison, secure children's homes and young offender institutions would have a far lower reoffending rate if the model of placing teenagers with criminal identities in institutions achieved desistance. If we want to be better at developing desistance for children looked after, we need to be having the right conversation about identity formation.

Although exceptions happen, they do not make the rule. Again, if I am right, this demonstrates that relational criminality is a stronger correlating factor for the development of a criminal identity which leads to prolific and serious offending than even early contact with the justice system. As we have found throughout exploring several studies including the Taylor review of the youth justice system (2017), early contact is also suggested to be significant. I do not believe the prison population of care experienced people end up there because they were criminalised early in a residential home, even at a time when early criminalisation was more prevalent. Of course, this type of behaviour management is unacceptable and will definitely cause a distrust in professionals and is poor practice whichever way we look at it. It just seems this is often a symptom of the issues, rather than the root cause, which is identity and relationships, human connections or lack thereof.

Exploring the link between childhood trauma and crime, Beyond Youth Custody in their report 'Young Offenders and Trauma' (Liddle et al, 2016) found that 91 per cent of the young people that were incarcerated had experienced abuse, neglect or loss. One adolescent serving a lengthy sentence told me that he 'did not have a rough upbringing.' Within a week of knowing him, I found out his father was a lifelong criminal and heroin addict, who abused him consistently and his aunt is also serving a lengthy prison sentence. Interestingly, I would have given the self-same answer if asked that question at 16, even though I score 9/10 on the ACE questionnaire and had lived in 18 different places before I reached 13-years-of-age, using heroin to help me cope.

I couldn't have possibly understood how my relational experiences and exposure to vicarious trauma of perplexed adults as a developing child shaped me or my identity and influenced my behaviour until I was a young adult. This is an example of the importance of relationships. It is trusting relationships that will allow young people to reflect and draw these conclusions by walking alongside them through the complexities of human life, not assessment, programmes or flipcharts, paper and pens. It will only feel safe to do so if they feel they have nurturing, caring, supportive adult relationships to help buffer the pain these reflections are likely to unearth. Programmes or assessment processes will always be limited in providing this level of comfort or safety and yet get far too much focus or merit at the expense of relationships within a criminal justice context. We develop inspection frameworks on what we can measure and then services focus on what will be inspected. In between this merry-go-round we say relationships matter but they will get little focus.

When thinking about the 'Adverse Childhood Experiences (ACE) Study' (Felitti et al, 1998), the most negative impact on development is not the adversity itself, as we have found, but the lack of supportive adults to help buffer the experience. The medicine of relationships.

If we explore adversity through this lens, although there are many critiques of the care system, when it comes to offending specifically, it seems to be helping many children desist from offending through nurturing adult relationships. It is possible that vast numbers of children are in fact receiving supportive relationships in the care system which prevents contact with the justice system.

The relationships they receive can often help reshape or redirect their identity, diverting them from the justice system. As all three interviewees in *Chapter 6* as young adults were clear, they felt it was relationships that made the difference, and many care experienced young people have their first experiences of a secure base in the care system.

The experience of trauma is of course compounded if the young person is unable or unwilling to receive the supportive relationships on offer. Many then move from placement to placement which can increase the risk of offending and they may also be provided with supported accommodation in areas of deprivation (Youth Justice Board, 2016). It is very easy to say this is unacceptable because it is. We must also have a nuanced discussion about resources because many of these young people don't like the care system, however many need continued support when they leave it.

The original ACE study does have limitations such as not considering pre-birth experience, as our brains develop from conception into adulthood (Siegel and Bryson, 2012). We know that there are 'key sensitive' periods during childhood and adolescence where children's brains are more malleable and, as a result, more susceptible to positive or negative experiences (Shonkoff et al, 2008). I score 9/10 on the ACE questionnaire (I completed the ACE test on myself to explore what I would score and to help me reflect when writing my first book, *Your Honour*). I do not advocate individual screening for children, unless there are mechanisms and structures in place to appropriately respond and those screened fully-understand the results are far from deterministic. The human experience is far too complex to determine an outcome in such a simplistic way. As I have already suggested, it does not capture every adversity, nor the relational support or capacity of the child to manage it. It was the institutional response of family separation and incarceration which caused the most memorable harm to me. The study didn't explore the adversity of societal responses to ACEs such as school exclusion, marginalisation, homelessness, prejudice, racism and custody but these cause harm to the mind and body.

At 17, I was incarcerated in a young offender institution and, although I had grown-ups around, domestic violence, abuse, neglect and criminality, this experience heightened my stress response system. Just on the way to the prison itself, my heart felt like it was going to give up on me. Was I going to be the smallest, was I going to be sexually-assaulted, would I see my mum or siblings again? As I was on remand, these thoughts were whizzing through my mind. All of them raised my adrenaline and cortisol levels and I hadn't even reached prison yet to witness the endemic violence between prisoners. I don't think I really felt safe for around two months and, when I did, it was because I developed strategies to keep myself safe which were often violent. Strategies that were paradoxical to managing regulated relationships in the community. My main topic of conversation on release was prison and crime as this had defined my early life. Of course, these are topics the average person avoids like the plague and when this is the only language you know it creates further relational poverty.

Although we have found that trauma itself is not a causal link to offending, it does of course have a significant relationship with offending in various ways, explaining Liddle et al's (2016) findings of traumatised young people in custody and Ford's (2019) examination of ACEs in adult custody. In his short video, 'Recognizing Symptoms of Trauma with Dr Bessel Van Der Kolk' (2015), he describes three adaptations of untreated developmental trauma in people as they grow as follows (paraphrased and expanded):

- Attention—an inability to stay focused on tasks for periods of time which inevitably affects a child's ability to engage with school as teachers require attentive children to learn. This would explain the exclusion to custody 'pipeline.'
- Relationships—if someone has been harmed, they will position themselves in the world to protect themselves. This may be by presenting as arrogant or violent or also being passive because this is an adaption to survive in an unsafe world. This is a perfect description of the many prisoners I met on my four years of travel through the prison system, from juvenile to adult. The adaptations to their environments eventually became an intrinsic part of their identity.
- Affect regulation—which he describes as the hijacking of emotion which impacts on an individual's ability to navigate events or self-regulate. This would explain a vast amount of conflict within disadvantaged communities when it comes to knife crime, gang violence and over-reactions to seemingly minor incidents. As suggested in the ACEs and Equality Window above, the children with

the least capacity to manage stress due to dysregulation are those most likely to be confronted with stressful events.

I think about regulation as like having a driving licence. If a parent doesn't have one they develop strategies to navigate traffic without it. This might not be too dangerous if you are in a suburban area with little traffic and 30 mph speed limits that most drivers comply with. However, when that parent teaches a child to drive in an inner-city area with chaotic traffic, duel carriageways or on 70 mph motorways, driving without a licence becomes far more challenging. Ten times more difficult if the parent is screaming at the child while he or she is learning to drive.

We as professionals are 'driving instructors' and our job is to recognise how such driving habits developed, accept the young people have them and then work with them to enhance skills or modify them. Disengagement or disconnection often happens when we don't recognise or respect the skills they have developed. To the young people, these skills can be everything. They only need tinkering with for them to become expert drivers on the roads they have to navigate. Remember, these roads are their roads which they remain on when we are no longer in the car. So instead of asking them to walk instead of drive, we must support them to improve the skills they have acquired, get a licence and break the cycle of poor drivers, thereby creating safer roads.

This goes some way towards explaining the lure of or connection to 'my boys' and the 'why' around my own exploitation (as more fully explained in my first book). My exploitation arose through my and my exploiter's inter-connectedness, interpersonal relationships and shared skill sets of navigating dangerous roads, without a driving licence. I shared experiences with my exploiter and it felt to me that we had a relationship that mattered; and I would also say we resonated. He presented himself to me as a role model because it felt like he understood me more than any professional or teacher that previously excluded me. Competing against this pull and sense of relationship is always going to be incredibly difficult for any professional. It is unlikely to take place in the context of programmes or intervention plans which is what the justice system has perpetuated for decades with offending behaviour programmes. This may go some way to explaining why other young people gravitate towards such relationships and away from professionals. They are unable to assess these older peers as a risk because they offer the skills these young people feel they need to navigate dangerous roads. We as professionals only judge their driving. Which relationship would you prioritise in their shoes?

Being born to an abused teenage care leaver affected my ability to self-regulate in dangerous traffic and believe me when I say it but on my roads most cars were stolen. My environment and relational adversities were so severe I was unable to cope which led to poor decision-making, lack of self-worth and addiction. Incarceration and the justice response only created further feelings of rejection, shame and guilt and this did little to address my ability to regulate myself or help me to understand why I gravitated to criminal peers and drugs.

The process is twofold. The social marginalisation that comes from being dysfunctional and dysregulated is one thing, then the gravitation to criminal peers through group membership and common behaviour and world perspectives is another. So, the experiences of childhood trauma play a role. However, alongside this, identity seems to demonstrate why this group of adolescents have the highest rate of reoffending and they are at risk of being criminally groomed. Therefore, when we say 'relationships are everything,' we are probably underestimating by just how much.

When we start to think about children who offend through this relational lens, we can start to recognise the very cohort of families most children incarcerated are coming from. They are likely to be predominately experiencing specific ACEs such as domestic violence, mental health and parental incarceration, although of course not always strictly parental. It can be other family members and peers, which an assessment is not always likely to draw out because it is often hidden in the background of a life story (like most of mine was). They are likely to have criminality either prevalent or historical within family relationships which plays a role in shaping the child's development. This inevitably develops into relational poverty and negatively affects the child's ability to develop regulation in a use dependant way as explained by Bruce Perry in his talk 'Born for Love' (2016).

If we do not recognise these experiences as our responsibility as adults, we inevitably create a narrative that blames a child for their inability to tackle trauma and adversity as well as having their identity shaped by adults. This can be tackled in a community way by not demonising these very children in the press and developing a prison system that is more humane and community-based. It is likely to cost money but the current prison system creates 'good prisoners,' not relational role models for children. Our prison system is far from being trauma-informed enough to provide opportunities for relational regulation. I believe we can have trauma-responsive prisons; we just need to start by changing the narrative of how we talk about prisoners, as a country. Spend money to save victims and build safer communities for children to grow. That makes sense to me.

So, when we ask the question as to whether we are helping these young people overcome adversity, or becoming a part of their fight, I believe that criminal justice, from top to bottom, needs to do both. Building awareness amongst staff is critical. Training practitioners in understanding trauma and the impact of trauma doesn't seem to go far enough. Training practitioners in the harm the system and the part they play in the process creates would need recognition in any trauma-informed training package as far as I can see. I have worked in youth justice for 14 years now and I have been blessed to have had that opportunity and work alongside some fantastic people. However, due to my duel experience and perspective, I have always recognised that I have become as much a part of the problem as I have the solution on a societal level. The best practitioners I have encountered on both sides of the justice fence (as described in *Chapter 5*) understand this complexity. They put themselves forward as people before practitioners and place connection before process, which is what Andrew, Luke and Atticus felt was important.

The 'Beyond Youth Custody' report (Liddle et al, 2016) on trauma states that 'Young people have detrimental methods of dealing with their distress and rejection of those in authority, these individuals tend to not engage with services.' The stand out words in this statement are 'authority' and 'engagement.' The justice system can seem blind to the impact of the power it holds over marginalised and vulnerable communities. Using words like engagement after incarcerating children from these communities seems to me to be inappropriate and institutional. If they feel harmed by incarceration, we must recognise this if we want to make connections with them; we must understand how they see us as professionals. The word 'engagement' should be changed to 'connection.' This way, both the child and the professional have a responsibility to connect rather than use a word that places emphasis on a young person to engage with the system that has just caused them harm through incarceration. Some may say they caused harm, which is relevant for retribution, but not for relationship building and reintegration. After a period of incarceration, punishment should be over, and relationships to improve former prisoners' future decision-making should be the focus.

Maruna (2010) in his work exploring desistance and redemption found two narrative scripts when interviewing active and non-active offenders. We have already explored these but not through a trauma lens. He describes those in the condemnation script as people that had little hope about their futures and were almost resigned to their life of crime due to experiences of poverty, stigma and criminal peers. He describes those in the redemption script as optimistic about their futures and, although they had offended, they were able to disassociate themselves from their behaviour psychologically. However, Maruna states that those that found redemption also believed they could 'beat the odds of the system that keeps people like them trapped in a cycle of crime.' Which is, by the way, not too dissimilar to my perspective of my journey to where I am today. I guess this is an individual's perception or interpretation of the word 'system' and the connection they have with it.

Maruna interpreted this as maintaining their identity, of being defiant against the system and simultaneously changing their behaviour. However, is it inconceivable that these prisoners were in fact right? Many prisoners have faced ACEs, complex trauma, school exclusion, care and drug addiction due to dysregulation and relational poverty. This inevitably limits their social relationships with people who could offer them a way out of criminality. They then enter a prison system that has a reoffending rate within 12 months of almost 50 percent or one in every two prisoners; highlighting recovering from incarceration can develop into a further adversity. Once criminalised, it is incredibly difficult to obtain employment due to disclosure requirements. Even a recent HM Prisons and Probation Service (2020) report from the very system itself states,

'Care experienced people may have experienced traumatic life experiences that can continue to impact them in adulthood. Before entering the care system, they may have been subject to significant trauma which can be exacerbated through the care system as well as the CJS.'

This is the system acknowledging *system trauma*. Therefore, I think it would be fair to say they beat a social system that was adversarial and unequal and now the very system itself is starting to acknowledge that.

We discuss privilege in terms of being white, middle class or male within society, however having a positive adult who can co-regulate so you develop self-regulation is essential to development. This could in fact be one of the most damaging disadvantages as it seems vital to the life course and relational acceptance. It is not a causal link to crime of course, however many caught up in the criminal justice system have not been provided with the start in life everyone deserves and requires to thrive. Not so much a privilege as a basic human need to function appropriately with crime just being one of many poor outcomes as a consequence. It could also explain part of the marginalisation of minority groups that are most likely to experience relational poverty and dysregulation through intergenerational trauma. Not that, e.g. racism, social oppression or discrimination aren't at play too, but if your access to regulated, nurturing adults is hampered by dysregulated, traumatised adults, you're potentially in serious trouble. This is not part of any discussion about disproportionality of those groups most likely to have had these experiences.

My interpretation of their view of the 'system' describes the society in which they have been raised and they place blame on authority due to its enforcement. It is, after all, the authority that leans on them with the hand of justice, post-trauma. For the 25 per cent of the care-experienced adult prison population at least, the society in which they have grown-up has offered little by way of relational buffering or connections. These prisoners often had service involvement from being very young, resulting in their expression of frustration, feeling let down by those they feel should have helped them. The blaming of the establishment is likely to be social programming and a result of viewing it as an entity to fear, not to embrace, leaving children growing-up with such adults at serious risk of similar world views. The developing brain has taught such young people to engage with their attachment relationships for survival and to avoid those they feel pose a risk to them, their families and peers. Forcing individual children to engage isn't the change required. Rather, how authority develops trust with marginalised communities that fear them is the change we need if we are to develop trusting connections with them.

The system in this context is the infrastructure that has left many children involved in youth crime to experience trauma. Then equally been ill-equipped to treat the child and help them develop the tools or self-regulation required to navigate society without contact with the law. Therefore, people like me, who have experienced significant developmental trauma, made poor choices and experienced incarceration, subsequently succeed, and we are entitled to believe we beat the system; please don't try and take that away. Even the young people in the 'Beyond Youth Custody' (Bateman et al, 2013) report also felt 'professionals that identified failures of services to deal with their negative earlier life experiences were more effective in relationship building,' indicating they feel the same. Whether others agree is their subjective opinion.

When working with individuals that have experienced severe childhood trauma within the youth justice system, guiding them to view things in alternative ways is only likely to be effective if it sits within relational trust and connection. Although well-meaning, challenge in the absence of such connection could feel like further exclusion from the young person's perspective and this is not a key principle of relationship building if a relationship has not yet been established.

Feeling safe and unjudged in relationships as Van Der Kolk indicates is essential to intervention because it presents safety to those susceptible to feeling the world is in fact unsafe and people are not to be trusted. We should be less interested in how we challenge the young person through programmes and assessment processes and more in how we build resilience or develop regulation which can only be done through relational and safe connections. We as humans don't respond well to being challenged by someone we do not respect or trust, or we believe lacks understanding of our perspective. This is being present enough in the relationship to provide limbic resonance and unconditional acceptance before any thought of changing behaviour. We as justice practitioners, however, trained to believe we can change behaviour through risk-assessments. This is why I truly believe the justice system is not as effective as it could be and in my view needs reforming.

Criminal justice has to exist and people of all ages have to be accountable for their actions. Victims of crime deserve a service that meets their needs and expectations. The question is, do those that change their behaviour have to view the system as their saviour? Do young people involved in low-level offences require a risk-assessment? What is the impact of risk-assessments on the identity of young people and children as low as ten-years-old? Have we ever considered how relational poverty feels for young people when the only functional adults that enter their personal lives only do so to define them through a risk lens as a result of their environment? The fundamental aim of the youth justice system is to prevent offending and promote the welfare of the child. These are serious questions we need to ask if we are to make young people that have faced so much adversity and trauma believe we are there for them, not only to change them. It is incredibly challenging due to various conflicting perspectives and maintaining public confidence in the justice system, I accept. However, we are moving further away from a punitive model to a rehabilitative one so we need to consider how relationships effect change and prioritise relationships over process.

If you are studying towards or working directly with young people in trouble, you may think these are structural issues that you have little control over and to an extent that is absolutely right. However, making the subtle shift from engagement to connection does ensure that the adult professional needs to understand their responsibility to connect with the young person and do all they can to recognise and reduce the disparity of power and complex barriers to become truly trauma-informed. It doesn't mean we can connect with every child, but simply recognising that, if we cannot, that it is as much the service we offer and how the young person perceives the world that is often the root cause. Not that they do not care because we all care, they just do not believe we can add anything to their lives, which is often developed through their own lived experience. If we better understand the complexities of relationship building with this group due to their complex lives and relationship with the system, we are better placed to develop limbic resonance. We are more likely to achieve the overall aim of preventing further harm and keeping young people safe with consistent, caring and nurturing relationships being the vehicle. This level of openness and limbic resonance may leave us feeling vulnerable, but it's the vulnerability that often creates the connections. After all, the young person is always vulnerable and often powerless when in contact with the justice system.

While in the justice system, we should support young people in trouble to understand how their brains and bodies have readapted to cope with living in unsafe contexts. Teaching children about their responses to trauma, social marginalisation or inequality in a child friendly way will not give them excuses for their behaviour. If that is the way they interpret this information at that time, it would just indicate their immaturity and capacity is limited, regardless of our message. However, when they develop, they will be able to reflect, ponder and draw their own conclusions about their decision-making in a balanced way that doesn't imply shame and guilt. They won't look at the system as one that simply wanted to change them, but also one that ensured they were aware that it *wasn't all their fault.* This would have been the most therapeutic thing any justice professional could have said to me. It would have made me feel that I was *seen* for more than my *behaviour.* That I was seen for my subjective reality which was that I was surviving a world of adversity and, although I was trying to be good, I didn't feel in control of the things around me as a child. Maybe even now I fall into the condemnation script?

As lots of the people in the prison system have faced childhood adversity, social exclusion and rejection by relationships that could have mitigated adversity, the system to them will likely comprise those that do not fit within their in-group. This is their own implicit bias grounded in their subjective reality of a society they perceive to be unforgiving, unsafe, unempathetic and even dangerous. I built relationships and connections with so many of these individuals throughout my prison journey. This is often why we didn't develop neural pathways of empathy or compassion as we didn't receive repetitive interactions that were empathetic or compassionate while our brains were developing in extremely important early years. While in prison, many prisoners with such experiences repeatedly tell each other that our behaviour is justified because the system was set up against us, indicating childhood trauma probably has a relationship with those prisoners that fall into the condemnation script. The job of justice professionals is to break down that belief with nurture and care using relationships and connections, not just through practice models or assessment processes. The justice system has to measure relationships in equal merit to processes. We must listen to those that experience justice from the inside. Relationships are just as important as process, so measure that.

Entering a justice system that has limitations in terms of providing relational buffering can contribute to a sense of demonisation and shame through risk-assessments, prison vans, handcuffs, cells and external controls. If we do not get the relationships right, the individuals experiencing relational poverty may believe, whether true or not, that justice professionals represent a group that only spends time with them because they're paid to do so. This is more than a derogatory label of being an offender; it's social rejection and a reinforcement of you as an outsider and it hurts, whether perception or reality.

For incarcerated young people, it's a case of breaking-down the barriers to provide consistent relationships and repetition of empathy, compassion and trust. Relationships are the most effective way to truly reduce youth crime. Prison or any secure setting, as I have found on both sides of this experience, do present an unusual opportunity if the relationships are right, due to isolation. In the words of Mother Teresa, 'Loneliness and the feeling of being unwanted is the most terrible poverty.' Young people don't feel seen or felt in a prison cell after facing far too much adversity. We should really listen to the message provided to us by the ACE studies of what young people say when they ask us to recognise how *we* failed them. This is simply holding us as a system account-able as we do the individual and creates some level of equilibrium.

Young people in trouble have often built and interpreted their resilience as fighting through a world they perceive to not be safe and have had to build resilience that looks different to others. As I have been told on several occasions by young people, 'Andi, it is what it is.' They develop their own strategies to navigate their real or perceived unsafe world which is often what brings them into contact with the criminal justice system.

Gravitating to relationships that they believe to be safe or familiar is not something exclusive to this group. It is a completely normal human instinct and goes some way towards explaining why this group often avoids profession-als. The feeling of shame and judgement is in part a result of being assessed as a risk. Professional relationships have left them feeling rejected and have been unable to protect them from trauma and violence in the past. They are not dis-engaging; they are often keeping themselves safe. We as professionals are seen as unsafe and not to be trusted for various reasons. Lived experience employees can really help rebuilding this trust in services.

When young people in trouble have experienced such adversity and, added to that, their attachments are to adults that represent a criminal identity, they become vulnerable to exploitation as active participants, as did I. Therefore, it seems that developmental trauma may be a correlating factor to the margin-alisation experience and factors that have a relationship with youth crime, but then relational poverty and constructed identity become more significant factors. This is often because their attachments keep them safe within the context of their world, even when it is deemed not safe by us as professionals.

In my experience as a young person in trouble and observing good practice in youth justice for over a decade, it is the practitioners that are trying to believe that the young people *do well if they can* in an unjudgemental way who are best positioned to influence change. The practitioners that are primarily led by process and risk-management which can be perceived as judgemental by the young person seem to have the least impact on relationship building. Again, relationship before process. Those that strike the right balance can become role models and walk down the path of authenticity together with the youngster. It is not solely about lived experience; this just provides validation within a relational context. Those without lived experience can of course obtain validation from the young person but it is not as readily available and often has to be earned.

Dr Gabor Mate in his talk 'The Need for Authenticity' (2016) explains how children suppress authenticity to maintain attachments to adults; this doesn't promote children to express their internal feelings. When young people within the system have had these experiences, trauma-informed practice is not only recognising their subjective reality and understanding it, it is taking a relational journey together so we can model authenticity for them. If we can persuade the young person we have taken that very journey, why would that not provide validation? This journey starts by accepting them without the need for them to be authentic and express how they feel. Only then can we hopefully take them on that journey to get where we want them to be. They may not have the motivation or capacity to be authentic and that is okay. After all, Maruna found that even those that eventually desist from offending believe they have beaten the system, so if this is how they feel let's make them feel they won. We should be more interested in being effective than right.

As professionals working with young people in trouble, we must seek to understand their subjective reality and make them believe we are in the fight with them, regardless of the gravity of the crime. This will help them feel *seen* and only then can we secure limbic resonance to help them construct the regulation they require to navigate their challenging, stressful or even traumatising environments. For young people in trouble with experience of developmental trauma along with a criminal identity, they are fighting to keep themselves safe and obtain a sense of belonging due to their experience of rejection, explaining their suppression of authenticity. The best justice practitioners can unlock the doors of distrust to create a relationship of safety for young people to start to explore their authenticity and express how they feel in unjudgemental spaces. If they can better articulate their feelings, they will likely be better positioned to manage stressful events or even say no when they are asked to participate in something they know to be wrong. Again, those that have taken this journey from despair to healing offer a unique insight into the tools required to navigate through this journey and through a lived experience lens.

We have found that there is a relationship between childhood trauma and those young people and adults caught up in the criminal justice system, particularly youth custody. However, we need to be careful we do not connect trauma with criminality. Much of the research we have examined suggests that those in the prison system, particularly those in youth custody have experienced severe dosages of ACEs and developmental trauma. However, in my considerable experience of crime, many people in society that commit it never or rarely get caught. This is often due to their social status, lack of contact with authority, involvement in less detected crimes, sophisticated methods and/or capacity to manipulate others into taking risks due to power. Therefore, we may fall into a trap of conflating youth crime with trauma as a result when the link is with who gets caught offending and those we incarcerate, not directly offending itself. I believe this is a flaw in the justice systems research.

Vulnerable members of society are often those swept up by the justice system instead of those responsible for drugs entering communities in the first place. These organized individuals made up a small proportion of the prison population during my years in prison and yet caused far more pain than those traumatised individuals that fell victim to circumstance and who made up a larger proportion of those we incarcerate. If this is as true generally, as I believe it to be, it tells us more about the system itself than it does about the disadvantaged members of society caught up in it.

I didn't meet many middle-class or highly educated folk on my journey through the justice system unless they were the ones sentencing, defending or reporting on me in court. I don't mean to sound flippant or controversial when I say such a thing or to offend anyone. It is just to make the point that, as far as I can see, the criminal justice system is functional if we want it to sweep up those in society with addictions, those that have experienced trauma and those that have grown-up in environments entrenched in criminality. Those that develop psychological, mental health or dysregulation issues that I now believe are more often than not grounded in their experiences of childhood. Of course, these are at times people that present harm through their dysfunctional or dysregulated behaviour and the justice system must keep people safe. However, we must always remember that the root causes of the behaviours are not only about life choices and that prevention will always be cheaper and more effective than cure. I was violent, dysregulated and offending before I even reached the age of criminal responsibility at ten, so the youth justice system was waiting for me and I embraced it as a scary but predictable life experience.

Young people, in particular, rarely commit crime in isolation which only further demonstrates the influence of their environment and relationships on their behaviour and choices. Trauma does not cause youth crime on an individual level; however, we would significantly reduce youth crime, addictions, anti-social behaviour and criminality on a societal level if we spent more money preventing ACEs in disadvantaged communities than locking-up those living with the consequences.

I felt ashamed of my relational trauma and adversity as a child, so I suppressed my authenticity to deal with it. Addiction and crime helped me bury it in a place so dark, it needed a gentle light from someone else's flame on their candle to help me find it again. I believe for young people like myself, practitioners in justice, care, mental health or drug and alcohol professions, will be more effective if we share our flame to reignite the flames of those that are in the dark. I rarely reflected or discussed it during my adolescence with professionals because, while being punished and judged, I simply didn't have the trust required to do so. In the words of Brene Brown (2012),

'If we share our story with someone who responds with empathy and understanding, shame can't survive.'

Therefore, if we alleviate the shame with our relationship, we inevitably reduce the risk of reoffending because we increase self-esteem and the likelihood of investment in ourselves and others.

CHAPTER 8

Relationships: The Key Components

This journey has explored:

- structural inequality
- childhood adversity (ACEs)
- Risk Relational Paradox
- implicit bias
- the Risk Switch
- relational poverty
- socio-economic poverty; and
- institutionalisation of the justice system.

These are all factors that contribute to the system's limitations in tackling recidivism. We continually discuss reforming that system as a result, particularly prisons. However, I am sure we can have a more productive justice system if we all place relationships at the heart of practice. As you reflect on this journey, you may consider aspects of it to be controversial, based on my own subjective bias, or even contentious. But I would suggest that we need to think outside of the box if we are to improve the outcomes of those individuals we are told cause us harm and for whom it is expensive to provide interventions. I outlined at the start of this book that I would ask questions of the system itself and, until we achieve better recidivism rates, we must be creative in looking for new solutions and understandings.

'Nothing Works' (Martinson, 1974), short sharp shock (Lotti, 2016), 'No More Excuses' (Home Office, 1997), offending behaviour programmes (Ministry of Justice, 2018), 'Scaled Approach' (Youth Justice Board, 2010), desistance, diversion (Tyrrell et al, 2017) and trauma-informed practice are just a few of the developments in criminal and youth justice over recent years. However, we have taken a journey which, I hope, explains how relationships in one way or another lead young people into trouble with the law, so improved relationships must be the most effective route out. This lens has allowed us to explore the complex relationship that young people in trouble often have with professionals and others; and the interface between the community and the 'justice system,' critically analysing how risk-assessment and the relational context of inequality and social status disparity, or power, influences those who work in it, and those that enter it as recipients. This is supported by research indicating that effective relationships are required to effectively change behaviour (Youth Justice Board, 2019). I have reflected my view of how lived experience in a criminal justice context can be a game changer when it comes to building bridges with marginalised communities and improving service delivery.

Within the exploration of the link between childhood adversity, complex trauma and offending, I suggest that it is the lack of supportive adult relationships to help mitigate adversity that causes as much harm as the adversity itself. If young people who enter the youth justice system spend a lifetime in the criminal justice system it may indicate they didn't receive the key relationships or attachments that could have helped them desist from offending. After all, they were children when the behaviour in question started. Just in the same way that Fellitti (1998) found stress and adversity can last a lifetime in the body, criminal identities constructed through exposure to crime, addiction and violence are just as difficult to deconstruct. This does not indicate the youth justice system is not effective, it just demonstrates the magnitude of the challenge ahead for youth justice professionals; one that should never be underestimated, or assumptions made that short interventions or even educational programmes are the answer. Targeting the pre-frontal cortex when the brain stem feels under threat from the system is unlikely to be effective without nurturing relationships. I believe that being available as a person is as important as any assessment, plan, intervention or supervision and this should be the primary focus of any intervention.

Martinson's (1974) paper 'Nothing Works' influenced criminal justice policy at that time finding that no rehabilitation programme was effective at reducing offending. However, within his conclusion Martinson stated that 'treatment programs are based on a theory of crime as a "disease"—that is to say, as something foreign and abnormal in the individual which can presumably be cured.'

I agree with Martinson in principle, that programmes or treatment will always have little effect on changing criminal identity. Identity is shaped relationally over such a long period of time. If an identity is shaped over years through relationships, a programme or short intervention is unlikely to change it, no matter how 'evidence-based' we may believe it to be. When evidence is presented, the effect claimed must be short-term if recidivism rates, as we have found, are as high as 50 per cent within 12 months of release from custody in the present day (Prison Reform Trust, 2019). It is only relationships that can have the desired long-term effect on young people's identity, therefore relationships should be the central focus rather than maintaining a fantasy of curing a disease which is in fact a community or social issue, not a medical one.

Prolific and serious youth criminality are behaviours developed through identity and relational networks that are often connected through the identities of groups within the 'village' that experience rejection and marginalisation. This identity, or sense of self, is in many ways shaped before the child has a conscious mind through relational experience (Siegal, 2017). Helping young people to make better choices, especially those who lack relational support will only be achieved within a relational or community context. It may be frustrating and slow, however forgiveness by a village that has for various reasons been unable to protect the child from the creation of the identity is the most effective approach to desistance for young people. That means we are all collectively part of the intervention because we are all collectively responsible. I believe restorative justice and prevention or diversion is the most appropriate justice response to reduce the number of young people in trouble with the law.

In the words of Perry (2017), 'The healthier relationships a child has, the more likely he will be to recover from trauma and thrive. Relationships are the agents of change and the most powerful therapy is human love.' It is a challenge to talk about love when young people enter the justice system for serious or prolific offending because the culture in the UK when it comes to crime is a punitive one. However, we must realise that the reason punishment is more often than not ineffective is because blaming marginalised children for being marginalised only causes further marginalisation. They are not simply making poor choices; their choices are often shaped by their environment. However, as someone that has experienced justice as a result of addiction, poverty and exploitation, I now understand that somewhere along my childhood journey, I lost any love for myself.

- If we want to teach children who offend not to repeat this behaviour, we need to use our relationships with them to help them develop a sense of love for themselves and a sense of belonging to their village, which will never be found in an assessment, plan or intervention.
- If the brain develops in a use dependant way, then let's use the neurons connected to compassion and nurture and flood them with practice of the very social skills we wish to develop in them.
- In the absence of loving themselves, young people in trouble often struggle to empathise with potential victims.
- Developing their ability to be authentic and express how they feel about themselves will be difficult to achieve through programmes or locked metal doors alone. This is more likely achieved through caring, nurturing consistent relationships.

The research we explored in 'Beyond Youth Custody' (Bateman, 2013) demonstrates how relationships help develop trust, and trust makes young people more likely to connect. Therefore, we:

- have to focus on training youth justice practitioners on relationship building with this particular group as much as delivering programmes or risk-management processes; and
- need to offer something uniquely different to teachers, youth workers, social workers and police officers that have come into contact with the young person and not been able to be that key relationship, for whatever reason.

Dr Bruce Perry (2020) in his video 'Regulate, Relate, Reason (Sequence of Engagement)' explains the sequence to engagement. He states that the best way to engage with someone's thinking part of their brain is to ensure they feel safe in the relationship which allows the information to reach the parts of the brain that can make sense of the information provided. I often pull on my lived experience to help me reduce the amalgamation of complexities and barriers to regulate or achieve that trust with this group. To achieve regulation as the starting point does take trust and this group is often distrusting of professionals, especially justice professionals due to a perception of enforcement, sanction and external controls. As James Docherty states (see *Chapter 6*), lived experience can get 'a whole gestalt in one picture.' This is often an automatic connection with the perspective of the individual in front of you. A recognition of how they view services or us as professionals. Then, as a result I can respond in a way that separates myself from the expectations they have of me as a professional. There are various methods such as humour, common narrative about something familiar to both or just how they may have been let down in the past and them feeling 'I understand as I have similar experiences.' Whichever tool is used in my case it was never trained. It is born out of my years of experience of receiving good and poor practice from justice practitioners.

Dr Sean Creaney (2014, pp. 102–125) found when exploring relationships within youth justice that:

> 'There is evidence that developing a trusting relationship is "effective" and that is a key component of effective practice, what is less clear is how to practically secure the engagement of a child.'

From my education, lived experience within the justice system and the connections I have made with young people as a justice professional in various settings, I'd like to suggest some key components. All young people are different and no practice model will work for all of them. I accept that. However, these adaptive and flexible key components provide the foundation for relationships. Relationship building and trust increases the likelihood of effectiveness of any intervention, practice model or plan aimed at influencing change as a key component for effective practice (Youth Justice Board, 2019).

Presence, attunement, resonance and trust

I first came across the acronym PART listening to Dr Dan Siegal (2017) in his talk 'How Relationships Shape Us,' while exploring how we develop our sense of self in the world through relationships. PART stands for presence, attunement, resonance and trust and is something Siegal used himself when working on a suicide helpline to build empathy and connect with the subjective experience of callers seeking support. He explains that he used these components when dealing with those at risk of suicide and realised that they helped develop relationships and empathy with patients.

I immediately resonated with PART, as a similar framework to the one I have used to gain trust from young people over the years by utilising my insight and perspective of lived experience. I have used these ways of relating to move young people from a reactive state to a receptive one by making sure they understand I see things from their perspective, making them feel seen and heard.

Replacing 'resonance' with 'connection'

The PART principles resonated with me as adaptable components which can be used to develop relationships with young people in trouble. I have slightly modified these elements and developed them into key components for relationship building in a youth justice context. The amended model can be remembered by the acronym PACT standing for presence, attunement, connection and trust.

Presence

What does it mean to be present or available for young people in trouble? It requires reflection, awareness and the capacity to explore the impact of Risk Relational Paradox and how it can limit our presence. As we have explored, there is a complexity within the relational experience whenever risk to others is prevalent. There is frequently an othering behaviour from both professional and young person, often implicitly. Reflective practice is imperative and asking ourselves:

- Where is our focus and attention?; and
- Are we available enough to align our presence with what the young person requires for them to feel seen and heard by a justice professional?

Atticus and Andrew in *Chapter 6* explained that it was the feeling that I was available for them that made a difference. They both stated that the worker's presence is what made them feel unjudged and created the opportunity for the relational magic to take place through a non-judgemental lens. I presented myself as Andi the human first that accepted them without the expectation of change; youth justice practitioner second, at no cost whatsoever.

To be present is to recognise their life experiences, not to patronise or pathologise them but to respect them. The key word here is 'respect.' But have we been socially conditioned not to respect people who behave in a way that harms other people? Everyone seeks respect, so we must respect them, even when we don't agree with their choices. We can respect the young people for being who they are and what they have overcome which is often the root cause of the behaviour. It is likely that we will not overtly discriminate, however offences or deviant behaviour naturally affect the way people relate or interconnect. Recognising how this affects our presence and availability to have an authentic and natural relationship with the young person is imperative. We must never assume that a young person being assessed as a risk will believe that someone doing that assessment is available relationally. Yet it can be achieved by helping young people to become aware that you fully-understand how they feel let down and that our plan is to assist them, not try to change who they are. Otherwise, this often feels to them as if the system has become a part of the adversity, and we must try to reverse this.

Respect that many young people who display severe behavioural issues and get into trouble have often experienced trauma, adversity and criminality which constructs their world view and relationships. Their presenting behaviours, although anti-social, are often adaptations and survival techniques required to navigate their environmental and relational adversities. This is why it is such a challenge to change their behaviour or identity; it is how they have managed to protect themselves from harm and so they will expect, as we all do, to be respected for their strengths. They have often been taught that authenticity is a weakness, and although we may disagree, we must respect and understand why. We can respect the decisions young people in trouble make without justifying their behaviours. If the young people feel we respect who they are, they are more likely to allow us to be present in their lives. Presence is the power of showing-up for the young person in a way that surprises them. Andrew, Atticus and Luke all desisted from prolific offending and went on to live non-offending lives, but not without several hiccups. In Atti's words, 'It was the informal relationship that made the difference.' Therefore, informal approaches are as important as our formal interventions, so we must focus our attention on that and this is how to be present and available for this group.

Attunement

Dan Siegal explains 'attunement' as the focus of attention on the internal state of the young person, not just on their outward behaviour. Being attuned to young people in trouble internally does not come without personal adjustment and effort. This is the step of meeting the young people where they are emotionally and ensuring they sense that they are being seen and felt. If the young person feels the relationship is superficial, they will not relax their stress response system, which is often on high alert in the presence of justice professionals. A contact based on enforcement alone will create a barrier to connection. Young people in trouble will not be emotionally available for attunement in this context. This is contact, but not attunement and doesn't present an opportunity for the relationship to blossom. Young people speaking to professionals about their negative behaviour is of course required in a justice context. Therefore, justice professionals often need to be attuned on an emotional level to young people to alleviate any feeling of shame or judgement they might hold. If we are attuned to the young person, it is possible to replace shame and guilt with belief and inspiration. This is where the impact of implicit bias or assumptions on either side can influence the relationship. Brene Brown (2013) captures attunement by stating,

> 'No-one reaches out for compassion or empathy so you can teach them how to behave better. They reach out to us because they believe in our capacity to reach our darkness well enough to sit in the dark with them.'

To achieve attunement it's imperative to understand the subliminal messages our behaviour projects towards those individuals that we are assessing for risk. Ensure they are aware that you will adjust your internal position to meet them in their emotional place when they feel emotions like guilt and shame.

By doing so, you can find the magical relational space of mutual attunement in the exact difficult moments that it is required, such as when you're discussing their offending behaviour.

The adjustment to attune must start with the professional when it comes to young people with traumatic experiences. The timing of asking challenging questions is everything for attunement. Justice professionals are required to ask personal questions quite early in a relationship, so presence and attunement are essential to building that rapport as quickly as possible. I often try to use humour or relatable experiences that they can visualise to overcome such moments. You may have different techniques that are authentic to you, however if the relationship feels superficial or solely based on intervention to the young person, attunement is far less likely.

Attunement also requires recognition of the relational disparity of power between institution and young person, as this is often the barrier to their availability for attunement. An adjustment of our approach in accordance with the young person's emotional needs is required, even if to state, 'This is not me, it is the requirements of me' to demonstrate our humanity. We should ensure we are able to navigate and support the young person through our processes when they feel they are too directive. Being attuned will help recognise that our system can compound their experience of relational poverty and feel adversarial. If a we are attuned, it can help first recognise this when it happens and then help us position ourselves in a way that allows the young person to feel assisted as opposed to directed.

Institutions or processes are rarely relational, we are. To mitigate against the inequality and intersectionality the young person has experienced and continues to experience within their relationships with the various systems they are navigating, we must adjust our behaviour so we are operating in the margins or redressing that balance of power wherever possible. The best tool to improve their behaviour is relationships and attunement, not a reliance on plans or objectives. These are important for risk-management and containing behaviour, but are likely to be ineffective in changing behaviour.

This does not mean colluding with the young person or not adhering to our professional expectations or service values, just recognition that the two things often need a bridge and this is the relationship. It means you are attuned to the feelings of being a young person caught up in a web of services which at times feels disempowering.

Attunement can often mean being open about how hard it will be to complete any intervention offered by our service(s). This will demonstrate to the child that you see them in a way that others may often have missed; and that you are *on their side*. It is vitally important to continue to reflect on the pressures of assessments, plans, interventions and deadlines and how they affect you personally and professionally. We are human beings and workloads affect us and that affects our presence and capacity for attunement with young people that challenge us in various ways.

Connection

Let's just get rid of the word 'engage' and replace it with 'connect.' Engagement is a completely inappropriate word to use when working with young people in trouble. It is used to place the responsibility on the young person for not connecting to an individual professional or service. If we replace engage with the word connect, we recognise the reciprocal process of all relationships. If we ask ourselves, 'Have we connected with that young person?' we then place a shared emphasis on ourselves to be present enough to understand the young person and place attunement at the heart of our practice to make sure we feel connected to the young person, and not the other way around.

Dr Dan Siegal explains this component in his PART model as resonance. To allow your inner state to be shaped by the inner state of the young person. It is not mirroring, but limbic resonance (Cash, 2011) which we first met with in *Chapter 4*, the emotional energy and connection between two people. The young person will feel an organic relational flow from you being present and attuned and you will naturally connect with them on an emotional level and the relationship will be more than just *professional*. Limbic resonance creates the connection which allows the space for Perry's (2020) 'Regulate, Relate, Reason' model to bloom. The young person can then develop empathy, compassion and patience through mirroring our behaviours in a use dependant way once they believe we are on *their* side.

Being able to adapt our relational style to connect with young people to take them on a journey as a role model is an underestimated skill. They are often seeking role models and, if we focus entirely on challenging all of their behaviours they will simply *other* us or place us in their out-group. It is far easier and less confrontational to challenge someone's behaviour when a connection has already been nurtured through presence and attunement.

Our role as justice professionals in the circumstances of a young person's life that is struggling with behaviour is simple:

- keep them safe and prevent them causing harm to themselves and others;
- assessment, plans, interventions and referrals will forever play their role, however they are far more likely to effect short-term change or primary desistance;
- for long-term sustainable change or secondary desistance, we are far more likely to achieve that through connection, not process.

This is what we found with Andrew, Atticus and Luke.

- Think bigger than risk-management and process.
- Think relational connection for improved life outcomes.
- Reflect on how to adjust our relational style to connect to them.

Many of this group have been constantly assessed through the Risk Switch and often with little impact. There is a difference between listening to young people for our risk-management processes and hearing young people and connecting with them. Once we're connected, the young person will feel seen and felt by that connection. When they feel seen and felt, we are more likely to be the person they call on when they need someone to assist them through their adversities; now that's connection.

Trust

The last but most important component is of course is trust. Without trust they say, we have nothing. It should never be a component we take for granted or assume is readily available from this group of young people. I have found through a lifetime of being involved in criminal justice in one context or another that trust can be found between professional and recipient but, for all the reasons outlined in this journey, it cannot be assumed that it doesn't need training.

These components interrelate and fluctuate but they are vital to gain the trust of those who have experienced significant relational poverty and often system trauma. Trust is what moves young people from being in a reactive state to being in a receptive state meaning the intervention, however that may look, becomes more likely because it is relational. Many have experienced the Risk Switch and will have a view that services for which we work have failed to protect them, failed to support them, and also demonised those around them. Again, recognising this is *not* a shifting in responsibility. If they have been left to survive adversarial environments, even though services have known about some level of risk, it needs acknowledging, otherwise we will lose any ground we have covered. 'We should have protected you from that and I am sorry' would have been a good thing to hear from any justice practitioner through my journey; instead of 'You don't take responsibility, Andi' which simply damaged my trust for professionals.

For this group, we need to move beyond simply assuming that the same approach that works for all other young people will work for them. It takes more than being genuine, honest, open and inclusive. This way of thinking is not backed-up by the fact that most professionals have tried these approaches and they haven't been effective. PACT ensures justice practitioners have a philosophy; a framework to building relationships which we have found throughout this journey is essential. However, if you follow the components of presence, attunement and connection, you will resonate with young people and build trust. That is where the change process is most likely to happen and, if it doesn't, you will still form a connection they will remember. You will develop the limbic resonance required to allow the young people to ensure you are the role model they feel comfortable with and, as a result, they are more likely to mirror the behaviours you model. But if a young person doesn't trust us as professionals, why would they mirror behaviours we are modelling?

With trust comes responsibility. Young people who have developed criminal identities in the midst of experiencing complex ACEs, relational poverty and developmental trauma are likely to struggle with attachment. They need positive relationships for them to thrive. Young people in trouble with the law require consistent relationships and human connections to improve their capacity to navigate their environments, especially as the world they often live in is fast moving and incredibly demanding. Although assessment processes, programmes, models or projects will always exist, remember, it shouldn't be a referral that can provide those special relationships, it should be us. Better framed as, 'Every interaction is an intervention' as per Dr Karen Treisman (2019) in her talk 'Relational and Developmental Trauma.' Also, in the words of Bessel Van Der Kolk (2015), 'Being able to feel safe with other people is probably the single most important aspect of mental health; safe connections are fundamental to meaningful and satisfying lives.'

THE ESSENTIAL COMPONENTS OF PACT

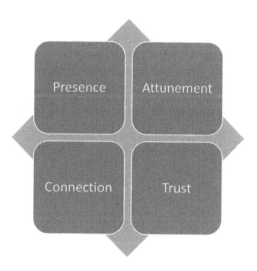

Siegal (2017), Shonkoff (2007), Perry (2020) and others over recent years have found that relationships buffer or mitigate adversity for young people.

Most young people will, with the relational experience, desist from offending, just like I did. PACT is a philosophy as well as a framework. It will help justice practitioners obtain connections built on trust. Young people are unlikely to remember our assessment, referral, plan or objectives. However, they will simply remember us, and role we played in their development through their adversity. Sometimes, all we need to do is make a PACT to be there with them, which as we have found is the most likely component to effect the change we wish to see.

Finally a Desistance PACT

- Some childhoods are characterised by crime and violence, and some children feel they have no alternative but to sit in silence;

- Throughout development, their behaviour can become their voices;

- We know punishment or judgement will rarely correct their poor choices;

- If we weren't able to protect them before, we should seek to repair that harm, not present them with more;

- Their involvement in crime lets us know how they feel;

- Let's make a PACT, let's be the relationship that helps them heal.

References and Bibliography

Bateman, T, and Hazel, N (2013), 'Beyond Youth Custody, Engaging Young People in Resettlement Research Report,' Nacro, ARCS (UK) Ltd, Centre for Social Research at the University of Salford, and Vauxhall Centre for the Study of Crime at the University of Bedfordshire.

BBC (2018), 'New body aims to get ex-offenders back into work': https://www.bbc.co.uk/news/uk-scotland-glasgow-west-44196724 (Accessed 9 August 2020).

BBC (2019), 'From Cradle to Care,' Nigel Richardson: https://www.bbc.co.uk/programmes/m000bb6w (Accessed 30 August 2020).

Bilson, A (2020), 'Born into care: Evidence of a failed state': https://bilson.org.uk/home/born-into-care/?doing_wp_cron=1604915014.6494710445404052734375 (Accessed 9 October 2020).

Brierley, A (2019), *Your Honour Can I Tell You My Story?*, Sherfield-on-Loddon: Waterside Press.

Brierley, A (2019), 'How Love Defeats Adversity,' TEDx: https://www.youtube.com/watch?v=U80R_ql8h7s (Accessed 28 August 2020).

Brown, B (2012), *Daring Greatly: How the Courage to be Vulnerable Transforms the Way We Live, Love, Parent and Lead,* New York: Gotham Books.

Brown, B (2013), *The Power of Vulnerability: Teachings on Authenticity, Connection and Courage,* 413 S Arther Avenue Louisville, CO 800727.

Brown, B (2020), Goodreads: https://www.goodreads.com/quotes/544060-if-you-trade-your-authenticity-for-safety-you-may-experience (Accessed 28 August 2020).

Burnside, J and Baker, N (2003), Foreword by Lord Woolf, *Relational Justice: Repairing the Breach* (Revised edn. 2004), Winchester: Waterside Press.

Case, S and Haines, K (2014), 'Children First, Offenders Second: The Centrality of Engagement in Positive Youth Justice,' *Howard Journal of Crime and Justice,* Volume 54, Issue 2, pp. 157–175.

Case, S and Haines K (2015), *Positive Youth Justice, Child First, Offender Second,* Bristol: Policy Press.

Cash, H (2011), 'The Online Social Experience and Limbic Resonance': https://www.psychologytoday.com/gb/blog/digital-addiction/201112/the-online-social-experience-and-limbic-resonance (Accessed 11 September 2020).

Centre for Justice Innovation (2017), 'Why Diversion Matters: A Briefing for Police and Crime Commissioners.'

Centre on the Developing Child (2020), 'Toxic Stress,' Harvard University: https://developingchild.harvard.edu/science/key-concepts/toxic-stress/ (Accessed 11 August 2020).

Cherry, L (2019), 'What Does it Mean to Have Resilience and Where Can You Buy It?': https://www.lisacherry.co.uk/what-does-it-mean-to-have-resilience/ (Accessed 20 July 2020).

Children's Commissioner (2020), 'Private Provision in Children's Social Care': https://www.childrenscommissioner.gov.uk/wp-content/uploads/2020/11/cco-private-provision-in-childrens-social-care.pdf (Accessed 11 November 2020).

Children's Society (2018), '7 facts you need to know about child exploitation': https://www.childrenssociety.org.uk/news-and-blogs/our-blog/7-facts-you-need-to-know-about-child-exploitation (Accessed 1 June 2020).

Clinks (2013), 'Just Do It, The Criminal Justice System Explained, Introducing Desistence: A Guide for Voluntary, Community and Social Enterprise (VCSE) Sector and Organisations,' p. 4.

Coleman, M, Doshi, S, Heynan, N, Bridges, A, Da Costa, D and Giles, D B (2018), *Relational Poverty Politics: Forms, Struggles and Possibilities,* University of Georgia Press.

Connolly, M (2017), 'Unlock the Power and Magic of Emotional Attunement in Your Relationships': https://newayscenter.com/2017/04/05/unlock-power-magic-emotional-attunement/ (Accessed 11 September 2020).

Cooper, L (2019), 'Our youth justice system discriminates against BAME children—and it's getting worse,' Centre for Crime and Justice Studies.

Courtois, C A (2004), 'Complex Trauma, Complex Reactions: Assessment and Treatment,' *Psychotherapy: Theory, Research, Practice, Training,* 41(4), pp. 412–425.

Creaney, S (2018), 'Children's Voices—Are We Listening? Progressing Peer Mentoring in the Youth Justice System,' *Child Care in Practice.*

Creaney, S (2014), 'The Position of Relationship-based Practice in Youth Justice,' *Safer Communities,* Vol. 13 No. 3, pp. 102–125.

Department of Education (2017), 'Children Looked After in England (including Adoption) Year Ending 31st March 2017.'

Department of Education (2018), 'The National Protocol on Reducing Unnecessary Criminalisation of Looked-after Children and Care Leavers.'

Dierkhising, C B, Ko, S J, Woods-Jaeger, B, Briggs, E C, Lee, R and Pynoos, R S (2013), 'Trauma histories among justice-involved youth: findings from the National Child Traumatic Stress Network': https://www.ncbi.nlm.nih.gov/pmc/articles/PMC3714673/ (Accessed 17 August 2020).

Evening Standard (2020), 'Rise in school exclusions linked to soaring numbers recruited by county lines dealers': https://www.standard.co.uk/news/education/bring-the-excluded-in-from-the-cold-rise-in-school-exclusions-linked-to-rise-in-recruitment-by-a4327276.html (Accessed 17 August 2020).

Farmworth, M and Leiber, J M (1989), 'Crime and Delinquency,' *American Socialist Review,* Vol. 54 (April).

Felitti, V J, Anda, R F, Nordenberg, D, Williamson, D F, Spitz, A M, Edwards, V and Marks, J S (1998), 'Relationship of Childhood Abuse and Household Dysfunction to Many of the Leading Causes of Death in Adults—The Adverse Childhood Experiences (ACE) Study,' *American Journal of Preventative Medicine,* 14(4), pp. 245–258, National Library of Medicine: https://pubmed.ncbi.nlm.nih.gov/9635069/

Firmin, C, and Lloyd, J (2020), 'Contextual Safeguarding, A 2020 update on the operational, strategic and conceptual framework,' Institute of Applied Social Research.

Firmin, C (2019), 'Contextual Safeguarding: Re-writing the Rules of Child Protection,' TEDx: https://www.youtube.com/watch?v=bCFZQcaIgDM&t=472s (Accessed 28 August 2020).

Ford, K, Barton, E R, Newbury, A M, Hughes, K, Bezeczky, J, Roderick J, and Bellis M A (2019), 'Understanding the prevalence of adverse childhood experiences (ACEs) in a male offender population in Wales,' Bangor University.

Friedman, S and Laurison, D (2019), *The Class Ceiling: Why it Pays to be Privileged,* Policy Press.

Greene, R (2010), 'Kids Do Well if They Can': https://www.youtube.com/watch?v=jvzQQDfAL-Q (Accessed 27 July 2020).

Greenwald, A G and Krieger, L H (2006), 'Implicit Bias: Scientific Foundations,' *California Law Review,* Vol. 94, No. 4 (July), pp. 945–967.

Hambrick, E, Brawner, T W B, Perry, B D, Brandt, K, Hofmeister, C and Collins, J (2018), 'Beyond the ACE Score: Examining Relationships Between Timing of Developmental Adversity, Relational Health and Developmental Outcomes in Children,' *Archives of Psychiatric Nursing*, Vol. 33, Issue 3, June, pp. 238–247.

Harris, N B (2015), 'How childhood trauma affects health across a lifetime,' TED: https://www.youtube.com/watch?v=95ovIJ3dsNk&t=570s (Accessed 20 July 2020).

Her Majesty's Inspectorate of Probation (2020), 'Serious Further Offences, Effective Practice Guidance, Serious Further Offence Reviewing: System Improvement,' p. 7.

Her Majesty's Prisons and Probation Service (2019), 'Care Leavers in Prison and Probation': https://www.gov.uk/guidance/care-leavers-in-prison-and-probation (Accessed 20 July 2020).

Her Majesties Prisons and Probation Service (2020), 'Working with People Who Have Experienced Care: A National Good Practice Guidance for Practitioners and Managers Across HMPPS,' p. 7.

Hocket, D (2017), 'We all have implicit biases. So, what can we do about it?' TEDx: https://www.youtube.com/watch?v=kKHSJHkPeLY (Accessed 30 August 2020).

Home Office (1997), 'No More Excuses, A New Approach to Tackling Youth Crime in England and Wales,' Cm 3809.

Home Office (2020), 'Criminal exploitation of children and vulnerable adults: county lines': https://www.gov.uk/government/publications/criminal-exploitation-of-children-and-vulnerable-adults-county-lines/criminal-exploitation-of-children-and-vulnerable-adults-county-lines (Accessed 4 August 2020).

Hopkins-Burke, R (2016), *Young People, Crime and Justice* (2nd edn.), Taylor & Francis.

Humphreys, K (2020), 'Alcoholics Anonymous Most Effective Path to Alcohol Abstinence': http://med.stanford.edu/news/all-news/2020/03/alcoholics-anonymous-most-effective-path-to-alcohol-abstinence.html (Accessed 5 August 2020).

Kolb, B and Whishaw, I Q (2009), *Fundamentals of Human Neuropsychology*, 6th edn. New York: Worth Publishers.

Lawson, V, et al (2018), *Relational Poverty Politics: Forms, Struggles, and Possibilities* (Geographies of Justice and Social Transformation Series), University of Georgia Press.

Lenkens, M, Nagelhout, G E, Schenk, L, Sentse, M, Severiens, S, Engbersen, G, Dijkhoff, L and Van Lenthe, F J (2020), '"I (really) know what you mean".

Mechanisms of experiential peer support for young people with criminal behavior: a qualitative study': tandfonline.com (Accessed 4 January 2021).

Liddle, M, Boswell, G, Wright, S and Francis, V (with Perry, R) (2016), 'Beyond Youth Custody, Trauma and Young Offenders, A Review of the Research and Practice Literature': http://www.beyondyouthcustody.net/resources/publications/trauma-report-research-summary/

Lochner, L and Moretti, E (2004), 'The Effect of Education on Crime: Evidence from Prison Inmates, Arrest and Self Reports, *American Economic Review*, pp. 155–186.

Lotti, G (2016), 'Tough on Young Offenders: Harmful or Helpful?' Warwick Economics Research Papers, No. 1126: https://warwick.ac.uk/fac/soc/economics/research/workingpapers/2016/twerp_1126_lotti.pdf

Malvaso, C, Day, A, Casey, S and Corradod, R (2016), 'Young Offenders, Maltreatment, and Trauma: A Pilot Study': https://www.ncbi.nlm.nih.gov/pmc/articles/PMC6818293/ (Accessed 17 August 2020).

Mate, G (2016), 'The Need for Authenticity': https://www.youtube.com/watch?v=pUGGNPAK6uw (Accessed 15 July 2020).

Mate, G (2019), 'Addiction is a Response to Emotional pain': https://www.bbc.co.uk/ideas/videos/addiction-is-a-response-to-emotional-pain/p07tnh6m (Accessed 1 June 2020).

Mate, G (2011), 'Dr Gabor Mate on Attachment and Conscious Parenting': https://www.youtube.com/watch?v=_tdljIW86e8 (Accessed 9 September 2020).

Maruna, S (2001), *Making Good: How Ex-Convicts Reform and Rebuild Their Lives*, Washington, DC: American Psychological Association.

Martinson, R (1974), 'What Works? — Questions and Answers About Prison Reform,' *Public Interest.*

McNeill, F, Farrall, S, Lightowler, C and Maruna, S (2012), 'How and why people stop offending: Discovering desistance,' Institute for Research and Innovation in Social Services.

McNeill, F (2006), 'Community Supervision: Context and Relationships Matter' in Goldson, B and Muncie, J (eds.), *Youth Crime and Justice*, London: Sage.

Merriam-Webster online dictionary (2020), 'Life experience': https://www.merriam-webster.com/dictionary/life%20experience (Accessed 19 August 2020).

Ministry of Justice (2012), 'Swift and Sure Justice: The Government's Plans for Reform of the Criminal Justice System,' Presented to Parliament by the Secretary of State for Justice by Command of Her Majesty.

Ministry of Justice (2018), 'Offending Behaviour Programmes and Interventions': https://www.gov.uk/guidance/offending-behaviour-programmes-and-interventions (Accessed 10 July 2020).

Morban, D A H and Cruz, N C M (2016), 'Copying the development: mirror neurons in child development,' *Medwave,* June, 16(5).

Moreland-Capuia, A (2020), *Training for Change: Transforming Systems to be Trauma-Informed, Culturally Responsive, and Neuroscientifically Focused,* Springer.

Murphy, D, Duggan, M and Joseph, S (2013), Relationship-Based Social Work and Its Compatibility with the Person-Centred Approach: Principled versus Instrumental Perspectives,' *British Journal of Social Work,* Vol. 43, Issue 4, June, pp. 703–719.

Oxford Academic, Social Cognitive and Affective Neuroscience (2017), Vol. 12, Issue 2, February.

Ozturk, E and Sar, V (2005), 'Apparently normal family: A contemporary agent of transgenerational trauma and dissociation,' *Journal of Trauma Practice,* 4(3/4): pp. 287–303.

Parliamentary Office of Science and Technology (2016), 'Education in Youth Custody,' Houses of Parliament.

Perry, B (2011), *Born to Love: Why Empathy is Essential and Endangered,* William Morrow.

Perry, B (2016), 'Born for love—Why empathy is essential and endangered' https://www.youtube.com/watch?v=5gU1wXbs5mc&t=1461s (Accessed 26 July 2020);

Perry, B (2017), *The Boy Who Was Raised as a Dog: And Other Stories from a Child Psychiatrist's Notebook—What Traumatized Children Can Teach Us About Loss, Love, and Healing* (3rd edn), La Vergne: Ingram.

Perry, B (2020), 'Regulate, Relate, Reason (Sequence of Engagement)' (Neurosequential Network Stress and Trauma Series): https://www.youtube.com/watch?v=LNuxy7FxEVk (Accessed 30 August 2020).

Pidd, H (2020), 'Youth Justice Board chair aims to tackle racial disparities in criminal justice system in England and Wales,' *Guardian*: https://amp.theguardian.com/uk-news/2020/jul/27/youth-justice-board-chair-aims-to-tackle-racial-disparities-in-criminal-justice-system-in-england-and-wales?__twitter_impression=true (Accessed 27 July 2020).

Prison Reform Trust (2019), 'Prison: the Facts,' Bromley briefing summary 2019.

Prison Reform Trust (2016), 'In Care Out of Trouble, How the life chances of children in care can be transformed by protecting them from unnecessary involvement in the criminal justice system, An independent review chaired by Lord Laming.'

Reavis, J, Looman, J, Franco, K and Rojas, B (2013), 'Adverse Childhood Experiences and Adult Criminality: How Long Must We Live before We Possess Our Own Lives?': https://www.ncbi.nlm.nih.gov/pmc/articles/PMC3662280/ (Accessed 22 July 2020).

Requarth, T (2016), 'Neuroscience is Changing the Debate Over What Role Age Should Play in the Courts,' *Newsweek*: https://www.newsweek.com/2016/04/29/young-brains-neuroscience-juvenile-inmates-criminal-justice-449000.html (Accessed 30 August 2020).

Restorative Justice Council (2013), 'Evidence supporting the use of restorative justice: https://restorativejustice.org.uk/resources/evidence-supporting-use-restorative-justice (Accessed 27 August 2020).

Rutherford, A (2002), *Growing Out of Crime: The New Era,* Winchester: Waterside Press.

Shonkoff, J P, Garner, A S, Siegel, B S, Dobbins, M I, Earls, M F, McGuinn, L, Pascoe, J and Wood, D, Committee on Psychosocial Aspects of Child and Family Health and Committee on Early Childhood, Adoption, and Dependent Care (2012), 'The lifelong effects of early childhood adversity and toxic stress,' *Pediatrics,* 129(1), pp. e232-e246.

Shonkoff, J P (2007), National Scientific Council on the Developing Child, 'The Science of Early Childhood Development: Closing the Gap Between What We Know and What We Do': www.developingchild.harvard.edu

Siegal, D (2013), 'Relationship Science and Being Human': https://www.m.drdansiegel.com/blog/2013/12/17/relationship-science-and-being-human/ (Accessed 3 July 2020).

Siegal, D (2014), *Brainstorm: The Power of the Teenage Brain,* TarcherPerigee, Penguin Group, USA.

Siegal, D (2014), 'The Teenage Brain': https://www.youtube.com/watch?v=TLULtUPyhog&t=486s (Accessed 01 June 2020).

Siegal, D (2015), *The Developing Mind* (2nd edn.), New York: Guilford Press.

Siegal, D (2017), 'How our Relationships Shape Us': https://www.youtube.com/watch?v=fwmtgrWKQrY&t=1562s (Accessed 9 August 2020).

Siegal, D (2019), 'Presence, Parenting and the Planet': https://www.youtube.com/watch?v=Ouzb_Urt7LQ&t=947s (Accessed 29 July 2020).

Sutherland, A, Disley, E, Cattell, J and Bauchowitz, S (2017), 'An analysis of trends in first time entrants to the youth justice system,' Ministry of Justice (Analytical Series).

Tajfel, H, Turner, J C, Austin, W G and Worchel, S (1979), 'An Integrative Theory of Intergroup Conflict: Organizational Identity,' in Austin, W G and Worchel, S (eds.), (1979), *The Social Psychology of Intergroup Relations*, Monterey, California: Brooks/Cole Publising Co, pp. 56–65.

Taylor, C (2016), 'Review of the Youth Justice System in England and Wales,' Ministry of Justice.

Treisman, K (2018), 'Good relationships are the key to healing trauma,' TEDx: https://www.youtube.com/watch?v=PTsPdMqVwBg&t=221s (Accessed 01 August 2020).

Thompson, N (2019), '"It's a No-Win Scenario, either the Police or the Gang Will Get You": Young People and Organised Crime—Vulnerable or Criminal?' *Youth Justice*, Sage.

Treisman, K (2019), 'Relational and Developmental Trauma': https://www.ageisteacht.com/relational-and-developmental-trauma/ (Accessed 5 June 2020).

Tyrrell, K, Bond, E, Manning, M, and Dogaru, C, (2017), 'Diversion, Prevention and Youth Justice: A Model of Integrated Decision Making, An Evaluation of the Suffolk Youth Offending Service,' University of Suffolk.

Tzoumakis, S, Dean, K, Green, M J et al (2017), 'The impact of parental offending on offspring aggression in early childhood: a population-based record linkage study,' *Soc Psychiatry Psychiatr Epidemiol*, 52, pp. 445–455.

UKEssays (November 2018), The Harmful Effects of Toxic Masculinity': https://www.ukessays.com/essays/society/the-harmful-effects-of-toxic-masculinity.php?vref=1 (Accessed 20 July 2020).

US Department of Health and Human Services, Centre for Disease Control and Prevention (2011), 'Cognitive Impairment: A Call For Action Now.'

Van Der Kolk, B (2014), *The Body Keeps the Score*, Penguin Random House USA; Reprint Edition (2015).

Van Der Kolk, B (2016), 'Recognizing the Symptoms of Trauma with Bessel Van Der Kolk': https://www.youtube.com/watch?v=rbqeGOXonUA&t=86s (Accessed 20 July 2020).

Webster, R (2016), 'Why Has Our Prison Population Doubled Since 1993?': http://www.russellwebster.com/story-of-the-prison-population-since-1993/ (Accessed 20 July 2020).

Webster, R (2020), 'Peer Mentoring in Criminal Justice': http://www.russellwebster.com/peer-mentoring-in-criminal-justice/ (Accessed 20 July 2020).

White, R, and Cunneen, C (2015), 'Social Class, Youth Crime and Youth Justice' in Goldson, B and Muncie, J (eds.), *Youth, Crime and Justice* (2nd Edn), London: Sage, pp. 17–30, UNSW Law Research Paper No. 2015–59, SSRN: https://ssrn.com/abstract=2657312

Widom, C (1989), 'The Cycle of Violence,' *Science*, 244, pp. 160–166.

Youth Justice Board (2010), 'Youth Justice: The Scaled Approach, A Framework for Assessment and Intervention.'

Youth Justice Board (2015), 'Keeping children in care out of trouble: an independent review chaired by Lord Laming Response by the Youth Justice Board for England and Wales to the call for views and evidence.'

Youth Justice Board (2018), 'National Protocol for Case Responsibility, Practice Guidance for Youth Offending Teams in England and Wales.'

Youth Justice Board/Ministry of Justice (2018), 'Youth Justice Statistics 2017/18 England and Wales,' *Statistics Bulletin,* 31 January.

Youth Justice Board Guidance (2019), 'How to assess children in the youth justice system': https://www.gov.uk/government/publications/how-to-assess-children-in-the-youth-justice-system/how-to-assess-children-in-the-youth-justice-system-section-4-case-management-guidance (Accessed 30 August 2020).

Youth Justice Board/Ministry of Justice (2020), 'Youth Justice Statistics 2018/19 England and Wales,' *Statistics Bulletin*, 30 January.

Youth Justice Legal Centre (2016), 'UNCRC report raises concerns for children in the criminal justice system': https://yjlc.uk/uncrc-report-raises-concerns-for-children-in-the-criminal-justice-system/ (Accessed 31 July 2020).

Zelechoski, A D (2016), 'Trauma, Adverse Experience, and Offending,' in Heilbrun, K, DeMatteo, D and Goldstein N E S (eds.), *APA Handbook of Psychology and Juvenile Justice*, American Psychological Association, pp. 325–342.

Index

A

abuse *133*
  cycle of abuse *148*
  intergenerational cycle *13*
accountability *92, 161*
adaptation *72*
addiction *11, 143*
adolescence *90, 134, 137–138, 151*
adrenaline *136*
adversarial system *177*
adversity *48, 61, 78, 103, 128, 134*
  adverse childhood experiences *134–145*
affect regulation *155*
age
  'age crime curve' *126*
  age of criminal responsibility *32*
aggression *15, 98*
alcohol *94, 135*
  alcohol abuse *135*
  recovery interventions *129*
alienation *30, 94*
anti-social behaviour *12, 30, 89, 151, 175*
arrogance *155*
assessment *38, 62, 66*
assumptions *176*
attachment *15, 30, 89, 96, 118, 134, 181*
attention *155*
attunement *63, 94, 142, 176–178*

authenticity *30, 83, 113, 118, 165, 175*
awareness *139, 174*
  building awareness *158*
  Risk Relational Aware *52*

B

barriers *56, 65, 75, 123, 164, 176*
belonging *22, 90, 103, 108, 118, 142, 149*
best practice *59, 76*
bias *59*
  implicit bias *12, 40, 53, 61, 163, 176*
  perceived bias *74*
  subconscious bias *152*
biology *134*
Black Lives Matter *40, 54*
blame *33, 79, 142*
brain *16, 29, 61, 70, 93, 125, 154, 160–162, 170*
  brain development *137, 140*
buffering *163*
bureaucracy *69*

C

care *34, 45, 59, 94, 101, 122, 143*
  primary carers *134*
  privatisation *152*
causation *11, 20, 71, 148*
  root causes *80*

Geese Theatre Handbook

Drama with Offenders and People at Risk

Clark Baim, Sally Brookes
and Alun Mountford

'A treasure chest of games and exercises for any group setting ... a wealth of food for thought ... for trainers of all kinds'
Criminal Justice Matters

'Fascinating ... Excellent ... If you're involved with offenders or other risk groups, buy it'
The Magistrate

'An absolute treasure trove for people who work with groups — in mental health, schools, training, social work — wherever'
Mental Health Today

Paperback & ebook | ISBN 978-1-872870-67-0

2002 | 223 pages

Fifty-Ones Moves

Ben Ashcroft

With a Foreword by Dr Peter McParlin

'A powerful book that gives a hard-hitting account of the care system ... and is vital reading for anyone wishing to learn about the true effects of multiple placement moves and the resilience it takes to "never, ever give up"'
Guardian

'Perhaps this inspirational memoir will encourage psychologists and social workers to spend more time listening to children and finding ways to build on their strengths and interests'
The Psychologist

Paperback & ebook | ISBN 978-1-904380-24-5

2013 | 148 pages

www.WatersidePress.co.uk

Your Honour Can I Tell You My Story?

Andi Brierley

With a Foreword by Jim Hopkinson

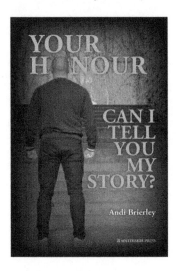

The challenging story of a young person's progress through care, prison and social rejection to youth justice specialist. It charts failures to connect with and modify the author's chaotic early life moving from place to place, school to school, fragmented parenting and poor role models. Encircled by crime, drugs and baffling adults, Andi Brierley ended up first in a young offender institution then prison where he learned to think like a prisoner for his own survival, making everything harder for everybody on release. Until he determined to change and put his past to valuable use.

'Wow!! I didn't put it down once I started reading!'
Lynda Marginson CBE, Director, National Probation Service (NE).

'Andi's compelling story shows why we should never
give up on the capacity of people to change'
Jim Hopkinson, Bradford Children's Services.

Paperback & ebook | ISBN 978-1-909976-64-1 | 2019 | 258 pages